THE MORTGAGE-BACKED SECURITIES WORKBOOK

Also co-authored by Andrew Davidson

Mortgage Valuation Models: Embedded Options, Risk and Uncertainty with Alexander Levin

Securitization: Structuring and Investment Analysis with Anthony Sanders, Lan-Ling Wolff and Anne Ching

Mortgage-Backed Securities: Investment Analysis and Valuation Techniques with Michael Herskovitz

the MORTGAGE-BACKED SECURITIES WORKBOOK

Andrew Davidson
and Michael Herskovitz

ANDREW
DAVIDSON
& CO

ANDREW DAVIDSON & CO

ISBN **978-0-578-14815-1**

Printed in the United States of America

This book is dedicated to the memory of

Kathie Hilterbrand Griffith

Acknowledgments

We would like to thank Kathie Hilterbrand for her careful reading, helpful comments and for actually doing all the exercises to verify our answers. (All remaining errors are ours.) Thanks also goes to Andrew Kalotay of Andrew Kalotay Associates, whose concise explanations of forward rates and binomial option models are the basis for Chapter 4. We would like to express our gratitude to emDASH for their fine design work and to Irwin Publishing for making this workbook possible.

We especially appreciate the efforts of Lan-Ling Milo Wolff, without whom this workbook could not have been completed. Her contributions included writing, editing, and organizing, as well as gentle prodding to keep us on schedule.

Introduction to the reissued edition

The *Mortgage-Backed Securities Workbook* (1996) was originally a companion to the book, *Mortgage-Backed Securities* that Michael Herskovitz and I published back in 1993. The Workbook grew out of exercises that we would require of new analysts who joined the MBS research department at Merrill Lynch. Analysis of MBS is all about cash flows; it was essential that our analysts could not just run models but also knew how to construct them. Converting cpr to smm and back again and knowing how to compute the difference between an ending balance and an amortized outstanding balance were necessary skills for understanding the results of any MBS analysis.

Through the vagaries of the publishing world (which I don't profess to understand), the *Mortgage-Backed Securities Workbook* went out of print. We were fortunate to be able to acquire the rights to the book some years later. During the intervening years, we have continued to use the Workbook to train new employees at Andrew Davidson & Co. The Workbook has also taken on a life of its own, with various people telling me about finding marked up copies and using them to learn the essence of MBS calculations. We have even seen copies selling on Amazon for over $1000.

With the release of my new book with Alex Levin, *Mortgage Valuation Models*, (Oxford University Press, 2014), I felt it was time to get the Workbook back into print. While many of the tools and concepts described in the new book did not exist and were hardly imaginable back in the early 1990s, the basic calculations have remained the same. The Workbook still provides a great entry into the world of MBS analysis.

Andy Davidson
New York
August 2014

CONTENTS

CHAPTER ONE

■

Innovation in the Mortgage Market

■

Susan Spring's determination had paid off. The Mortgage-Backed Securities (MBS) market did hold many wonderful opportunities. After her well-crafted presentation to her boss, Bill Stone, and the rest of the Fixed-Income Investment Strategy Committee, the group decided to make their initial foray into the MBS market. Susan was allowed to move 5% of the domestic fixed-income portfolio into MBS. She was told to keep the investments simple, basically PAC bonds and passthroughs.

The commitment proved to be successful since MBS did very well. The MBS sector outperformed the Treasury sector by nearly 100 basis points. Now, Susan was coming back to the Strategy Committee to request an increased exposure to the market. This time Susan was going for the big win; she was requesting that the allocation to MBS be upped to 30%, roughly its proportion of the domestic debt market. To get this proposal through, she was going to have to both convince her peers and then develop the tools to manage an even larger and more complicated portfolio. If this went well, Susan would be on her way to heading the Strategy Committee.

■ EXPECTED BACKGROUND OF READER

The reader of this book is assumed to have some exposure to financial markets, including the bond market. The basic concepts of finance and investing, including the structure of capital markets and discounted cashflows, should be familiar. All of the specialized mortgage terminology is defined in the workbook.

The book is intended for participants in the mortgage-backed securities market who are making investment decisions or aiding others in making investment decisions. Many of the tools described in the workbook are readily available from various vendors. This book serves to build a foundation for better use and understanding of these tools. The models described in the book have been simplified to facilitate the learning process. Investors should strive to build upon the knowledge gained here in understanding the more sophisticated analyses available.

■ WORKBOOK ORGANIZATION

This workbook was designed to accompany Davidson and Herskovitz's *Mortgage-Backed Securities: Investment Analysis and Advanced Valuation Techniques* (Probus, 1994). The chapters of the workbook follow the outline of the text. Although it is not essential to an understanding of this workbook, we highly recommend that you read the text in conjunction with the workbook as you do the exercises. The MBS book contains more detail and a fuller explanation of the concepts contained in the workbook, as well as a description of the framework which the exercises complement.

The workbook provides a multitrack approach to developing the key concepts. In each chapter, there is a brief description of each concept with relevant definitions and equations. These concepts are reinforced through numerical examples. Then, two levels of exercises are provided.

The first level exercises are designed to form a basic understanding and can be done easily with just paper, a pencil, and perhaps a calculator. These exercises can be identified by the icon in the margin.

The second-level exercises are more complex and should be done on a spreadsheet, such as Microsoft Excel™ or Lotus 1-2-3,™ also indicated by the icon in the margin. These exercises will build upon one another, so in order to do these, one must go through the chapters of the workbook in consecutive order. Though the spreadsheet exercises are not necessary to grasp the fundamental concepts, they will enable the reader to have a fuller understanding of the complexities of mortgage valuation. The answers to the exercises are at the end of each chapter.

Lastly, we have included some questions for review as well as some issues to think about. These questions will *not* have written answers at the end of the chapter; they will be marked by the icon in the margin.

■ HISTORICAL OVERVIEW

Mortgages are a central part of American life. About two-thirds of the families in the United States own a home through mortgage financing. Mortgages were traditionally financed through deposits in financial institutions, primarily local thrift institutions such as savings and loan associations, that hold the mortgages they originate. The domination of mortgage originations by savings and loans (S&Ls) is shown in Figure 1-1. Life insurance companies contributed to mortgage capital by holding large portfolios of mortgages. Supplementing the thrift organizations, mortgage bankers developed the resale mortgage market by originating loans to sell to investors.

Figure 1-1[1]

S&Ls Dominate Mortgage Originations in 1983

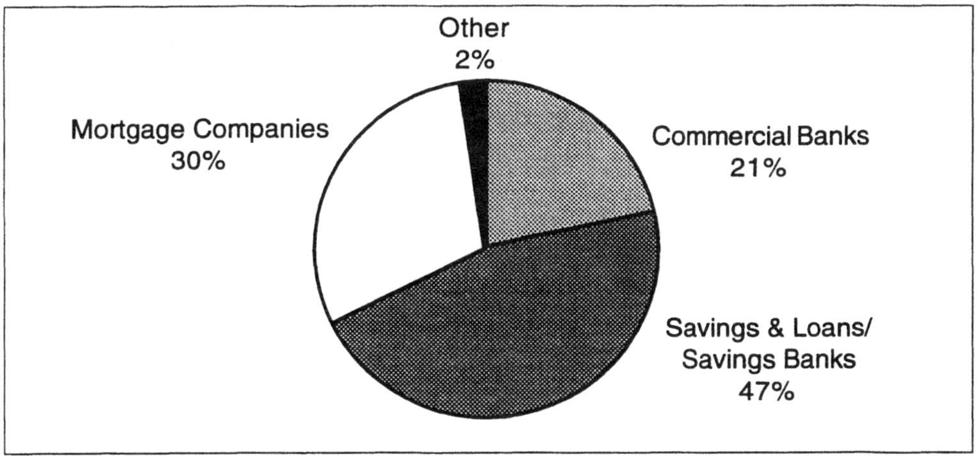

Figure 1-2

S&Ls' Market Share Falls to Less than 20% by 1995

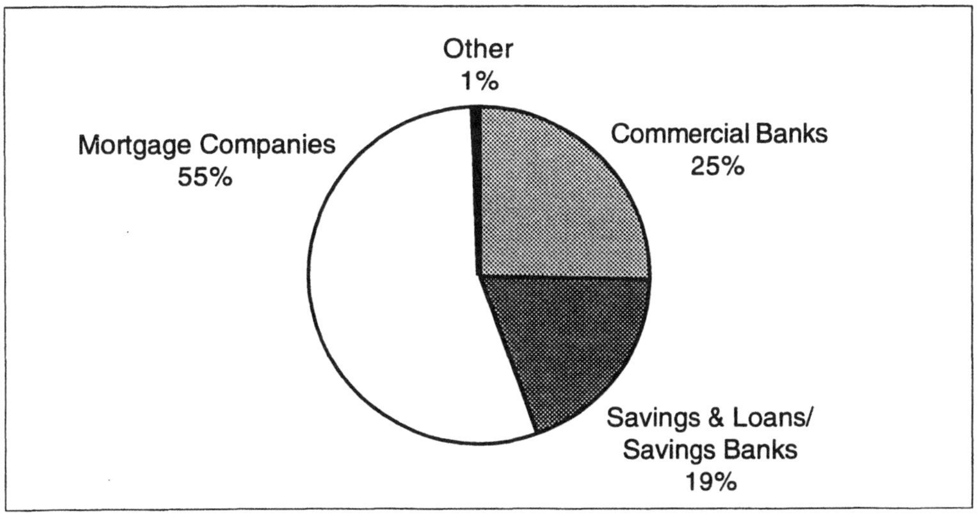

Jointly, the thrift institutions and mortgage bankers constituted the bulk of the mortgage market until the 1970s. At this time, interest

[1]Figures 1-1 through 1-5 are reprinted with permission of Inside Mortgage Finance, *The Mortgage Statistical Annual*, Copyright 1995, Bethesda, Maryland.

rates rose higher than the legal maximum on deposits, exposing the thrift institutions to disintermediation. The depositors diverted funds away from the thrift institutions into other higher-rate money-market investments. The thrifts' only recourse was to reduce lending and sell off mortgages. However, the high prevailing interest rates meant that mortgages had to be sold at a loss. This resulted in numerous institutions becoming financially insolvent and led to the S&L crisis of the 1980s. The thrifts' dilemma showed the need for an active secondary market where mortgages could be sold on a continual basis, rather than as an emergency measure. By 1995 the composition of the mortgage origination market had changed drastically, as shown in Figure 1-2. Mortgage companies that specialize in origination and servicing hold over 50% of the origination market. Commercial banks are rapidly gaining market share while the traditional role of the S&Ls has fallen to less than 20% of market share.

The growth of the secondary market in the 1970s was boosted by the Government National Mortgage Association (GNMA), the Federal Home Loan Mortgage Corporation (FHLMC), and Federal National Mortgage Association (FNMA). The three entities provided support for the mortgage market through the direct or implied credit of the United States, and created a standard for mortgage contracts through their mortgage purchasing programs.

Figure 1-3
The Growth of Mortgages and MBS

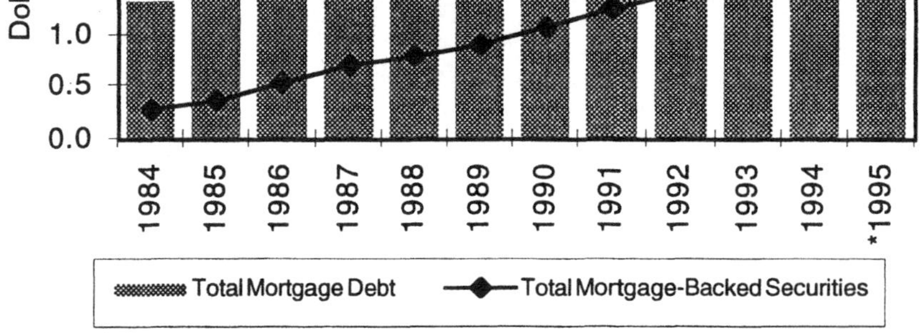

*First three quarters of 1995 only

The first mortgage-backed security (MBS) was introduced by GNMA in 1970. Since then, the MBS market has grown to over $1.6 trillion.

The growth of the MBS market is shown in Figure 1-3. Mortgage-backed securities created a demand for mortgages that increased the available funds for mortgages. The success of MBS can be attributed to its efficiency in reducing risk through diversification, and the sheer size of the market.

Figure 1-4
CMO Issuance

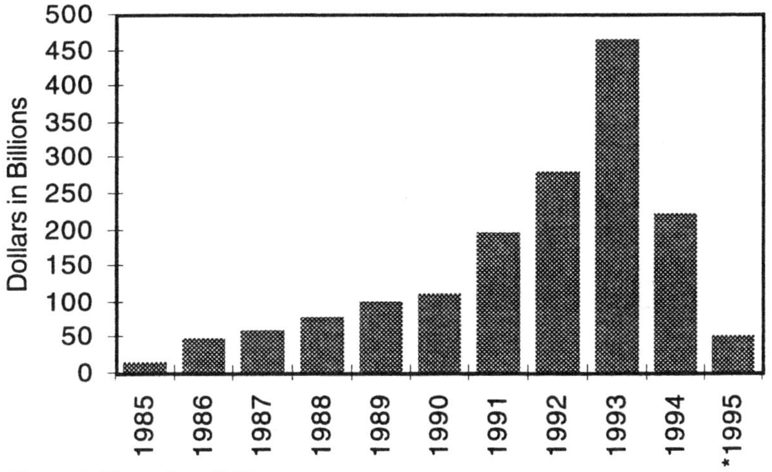

*Through November 1995

The first collateralized-mortgage obligation (CMO) was created in 1983. Wall Street took advantage of arbitrage opportunities in the huge mortgage market in an attempt to create value through carving up mortgage cashflows. The growth of the CMO market is shown in Figure 1-4. Wall Street enlarged the mortgage playing field by creating different types of securities from mortgage collateral. Instead of the traditional 30-year fixed-rate mortgage, investors could now pick from a seemingly unlimited range of bond characteristics. CMOs came in a variety of structures, maturity, and risk. In 1994, the dramatic turnaround in interest rates coupled with market uncertainty led to massive price drops in MBS. The negative publicity from a few well-publicized losses dramatically reduced CMO issuance. The diversity of the mortgage market is one of the reasons for its success but the complexity has taken many unwary investors by surprise.

Diversity in the mortgage market is not limited to CMO tranches. Originators competing for borrowers continually create new forms of mortgage contracts to meet the demands of increasingly financially savvy homeowners. The growth in adjustable-rate mortgage securities (ARMs), shown in Figure 1-5, reflects this trend.

The principles that have guided the mortgage-backed securities market have influenced the development of other asset-backed securities markets.

Credit cards, auto loans, home equity loans, manufactured housing, commercial mortgages, and even more exotic markets such as export receivables are all being securitized. The analytical tools described in this workbook will also provide insight into understanding these markets.

Figure 1-5
ARM Securities Outstanding

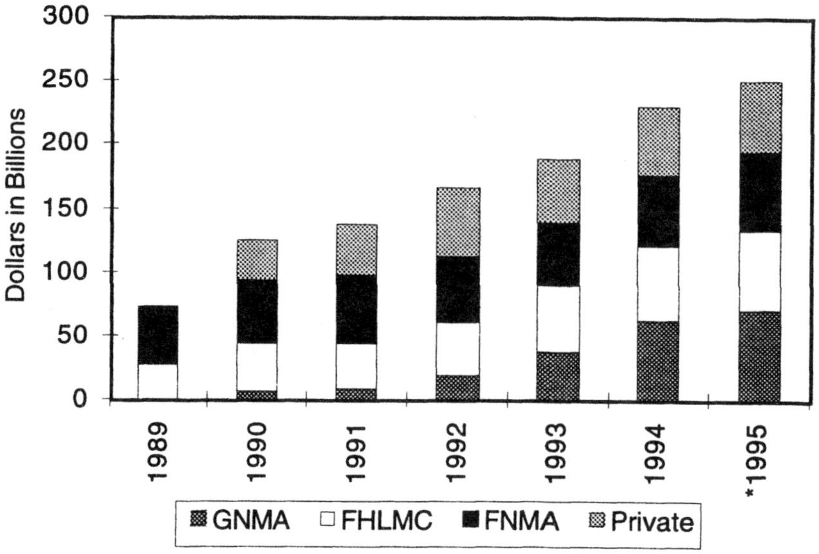

*First half of 1995 only

■ WHO GETS THE PIE?

The creation of a mortgage-backed security involves a number of players. First there is the borrower who wants a loan to buy a home. The borrower goes to the mortgage broker who arranges with a mortgage banker to originate the loan. The mortgage banker will securitize the loans. The security is sold to a dealer who will structure the MBS into a CMO or sell the MBS outright to a number of investors. Each of the intermediaries between the borrower and the final investor earns a portion of the proceeds. This breakdown is shown in Figure 1-6.

Once the loan has been originated, the proud homeowner will pay a monthly payment of principal and interest as determined by the loan contract. The loan servicer receives this payment and distributes it to the appropriate parties. The composition of the interest payment is shown in Figure 1-7. The servicer handles all of the paperwork for the loan and is in charge in the event of a default or prepayment. There are guarantees either at the loan or pool level by a government entity such as the Veteran's Administration (VA) or by a private guarantor. Both the servicer and guarantor will take as payment a percentage of the interest received from the borrower. The fees vary but are in the range of 20 to 75 basis points.

Figure 1-6
Who Gets the Price (Proceeds)?

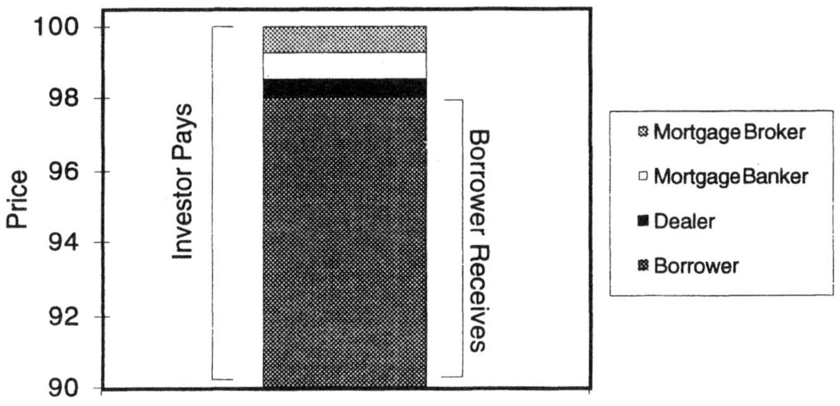

The net interest, that is the gross interest payment from the borrower minus the servicing and guarantee fees, is received by the MBS investor. The net interest can be further broken down into four categories. The largest is the funding cost which is what the investor could get from investing in an alternative short-term risk-free instrument. The duration cost is the further yield the investor gets for investing in a long-term instrument since a standard mortgage has an average life ranging from 5 to 10 years. The option cost compensates the investor for the prepayment risk. And finally, the spread acts as a sweetener to induce the investor to take the risk of a MBS over a risk-free instrument such as a Treasury bond.

Figure 1-7
Who Gets the Interest?

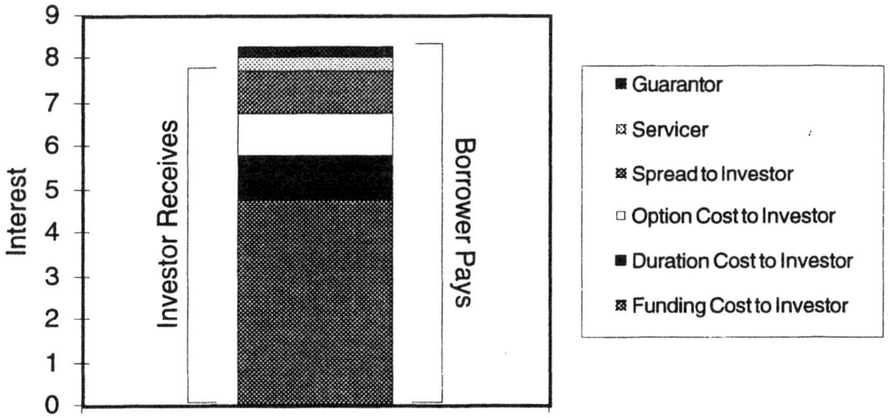

■ CONCLUSION

Innovation is the byword of the mortgage market. From individual mortgage contracts to multilayered CMOs, the participants in the mortgage market continually try to create new value and compartmentalize risk to meet the changing expectations and requirements of investors. This workbook is designed to give the reader a basic understanding of the mortgage market as it is today, and to lay a groundwork of tools and skills with which to attack the challenges of tomorrow.

CHAPTER TWO

Overview of the Method

The meeting started out fine. Susan Spring presented her plans for increasing the size and scope of the MBS exposure. Bill Stone acknowledged that the MBS sector had done well but did not feel comfortable with such a large allocation to MBS. Some Committee members, perhaps fearful for their jobs, argued that MBS were too complicated. Susan indicated that the Domestic Fund was in the bottom quartile based on five-year performance. This was attributable to the lack of MBS exposure, she argued. This point carried the day and the Committee authorized a partial increase to the exposure; MBS could comprise up to 20% of the Domestic Fund. Susan was allowed to move into all aspects of the passthrough and CMO market. Not a complete victory, Susan thought, but a strong vote of confidence.

■ FRAMEWORK FOR ANALYSIS

This workbook presents a basic framework for evaluating mortgage-backed securities: environment, prepayments, cashflow, and analytics. The framework is outlined in Table 2-1. Building a model for MBS is akin to building a house: if the foundation is weak, regardless of how elaborate the house is on top, it probably will not outlive a big earthquake. Thus, the results of any analytics rest on the environmental assumptions. The environment drives the prepayment model, which defines the cashflows. Only when these steps have been done with care can useful results be obtained from the analytics. A good analyst understands the limitations of the foundation.

Environment

The first phase, environment, is the foundation of any modeling and analytics. The environment specifies the range and limitations of the final analysis. Factors left out in this phase will not be considered in the final analysis. The most influential environmental factor is the level of interest rates. The level of interest rates drives the homeowner's incentive to refinance and also affects the valuation of cashflows. Interest rate assumptions range from the very simple where rates are assumed to stay constant throughout time, to the very complex where rates are generated by a two-factor log-normal, mean-reverting process, which satisfies a no-arbitrage condition and whose variance and covariances are consistent with historical observation.

Table 2-1
Framework for Analysis

Phase of Analysis	Components	Discussed in Chapters
Environment	Interest Rate Economy Supply/Demand Regulatory/Tax/ Accounting	Chapter 4
Prepayments	Environmental Factors Modeling Approach	Chapter 5
Cashflow Structures	Mortgage MBS CMO/REMIC Portfolio	Chapter 6
Analysis	Valuation Risk Income	Chapters 3, 7, 8, 9, 10
Full Process of the Four Phases	Environment Prepayment Cashflow Analysis	Chapters 3, 7, 8, 9, 10

While interest rates are undeniably the most important, there are other factors that drive the cashflows of the underlying mortgages. We like to call MBS "warm-blooded securities" because MBS are influenced by all of the factors that influence homeowners. Any changes in the homeowner's life, whether it be income and employment or marriage and children, will affect borrower behavior. These types of individual decisions are difficult to quantify. However, since an MBS is a pool of many mortgages, the decisions of one borrower do not significantly impact the security. Analysts use economic data on employment and housing markets to predict the combined impact of these individual decisions.

Prepayments

Mortgages have a unique characteristic that distinguishes them from other fixed-income investments: prepayments. Under the standard mortgage contract, the borrower has the right to prepay a mortgage, either in part or in full, at any time during the life of the loan, usually without having to pay a penalty. This right means that the investor in a mortgage cannot know the maturity of the loan or the amount of total interest that will be received with certainty. It is this uncertainty that is the source of risk and reward in the mortgage market.

Quantifying prepayment risk is the never-ending task of Wall Street analysts. There are three basic reasons for prepayments: moving, refinancing, and default. Since most MBS have some sort of guarantee on principal, the investor realizes a default as a prepayment. The assumptions in the environment phase will drive the prepayments. Prepayments are usually quantified in two main forms: forecasts and models. A prepayment forecast is a specific numerical statement of future expected prepayment levels given a specific environment. A model, on the other hand, takes the form of mathematical equations that relate environmental assumptions to prepayment rates.

Cashflow

Cashflows form the basis for any analytics. All analytics attempt to summarize the characteristics of cashflow. Calculation of cashflow is perhaps the most straightforward phase analytically, but may be the most time consuming. Cashflow calculations are another building block process. The MBS cashflows are determined by the pool of mortgages. The CMO cashflows are based on the underlying MBS. Portfolio cashflows are based on the cashflows of the CMOs, MBS, and other securities in the portfolio.

The greatest complexity in this phase is in gathering the appropriate data that describes the mortgages. Each mortgage pool has unique characteristics that determine the cashflow. Another important consideration is the level of detail. Loan-level information is not available to investors for agency-guaranteed securities; so most analysis is based on weighted-average characteristics of the mortgage pools. As in all of the phases, there is a trade-off between additional accuracy and computational efficiency.

Analytics

The summary measures produced in the analytics phase provide insight into valuation, risk, and income. Valuation measures indicate the relative richness or cheapness of a security. Risk measures provide a guide to the range of outcomes for an investment. Finally, income measures indicate the pattern of possible future cashflows. These measures serve as a guide for comparison to other investment alternatives given investment objectives.

The accuracy and limits of these measures are bounded by the full analysis process. The performance indicated by the measures is a direct function of the assumptions in the environment and prepayment phases that are reflected in the cashflows and summarized in the analytics. If a static environment is assumed, the analytics produced will not inform the investor of the probable outcomes should interest rates move.

WHAT THE READER SHOULD HAVE LEARNED AFTER COMPLETING THE WORKBOOK

Chapter 3: Static analysis includes much of the basic MBS vocabulary and involves all four phases of analysis at the most simplistic level. The reader should gain a basic understanding of the workings of MBS and cashflows.

Chapter 4: This chapter lays the groundwork for more sophisticated environmental assumptions. Yield-curve calculations such as forward rates, the par-yield curve, and the zero-coupon curve are demonstrated. The reader will learn how to build a binomial tree and be introduced to option valuation.

Chapter 5: Prepayments and prepayment modeling are outlined. The reader will understand the elements involved in prepayment modeling. The analysis of prepayment data is stressed.

Chapter 6: MBS cashflows form the basis for understanding complex CMOs. The reader will create CMOs using a simplified approach that will show the main principles. A spreadsheet model can be built using the concepts developed in previous chapters.

Chapter 7: Relaxing the assumption of an unchanging environment and exploring the time dimension of returns are tackled in scenario analysis. Changing environments lead to analytical measures such as total return, effective duration, and convexity.

Chapter 8: This chapter combines concepts of earlier chapters and demonstrates how yield curve assumptions affect MBS cashflows and analytics. Common spread measures are introduced.

Chapter 9: The Option-Adjusted Spread (OAS) approach to valuation is discussed. The relationship between binomial and Monte Carlo analysis is explored, and a simple OAS model is constructed. OAS results are also discussed.

Chapter 10: Two common regulatory tests are demonstrated: FLUX and FFIEC tests. These measures involve variants of the scenario analysis method introduced in Chapter 7.

■ CONCLUSION

Running the most sophisticated OAS models and looking at the entire gamut of analytics are not a substitute for understanding one's own investment objectives. Only when investment objectives have been clearly defined, in terms of risk tolerance and cashflow needs, can an appropriate investment be selected. Your analytics may tell you that a 30-year FNMA 6.0 is selling at cheap levels, but if you are using this 30-year bond to support a debt that demands a floating rate linked to the three-month LIBOR, the FNMA cashflows would be a poor match to your liabilities.

Good MBS analysis requires matching the solution to the problem. In the following chapters, we will describe and show examples of a wide range of tools for analyzing MBS in our four-phase framework. We will show where and why the tools are effective and how they fall short. Open-ended questions will give the reader a feel for the complexities and issues in the MBS market that are beyond the scope of this workbook. Working through examples and concrete problems, we hope the reader will gain further insight into the methodology for choosing the right tools and learn the skills to develop tools according to the reader's unique requirements.

CHAPTER THREE

Applying the Framework: Static Analysis

Another case of Murphy's law in Susan's quest to get a higher exposure to MBS: an interesting bid list of seasoned MBS needed to be analyzed and Jerry Garcia had just died. Not that Sue really had any emotional ties to the Grateful Dead, but the intense retrieval of information about Garcia had brought down the Bloomberg system. This hadn't happened since John Wayne Bobbit. To get the bonds analyzed now would mean only one thing—setting up a simple calculator using a spreadsheet. Good thing Susan had spent the time in the past to actually derive MBS cashflows and build some simple tools of her own.

■ INTRODUCTION

This chapter develops key building blocks in analyzing MBS. In particular, we cover prepayment rates, mortgage cashflows, balance, yield, and static risk measures. Development of the fundamentals in this section will be necessary for the more advanced analysis later in the workbook. At the conclusion of this chapter, you should have a firm grounding in the fundamentals of mortgage math.

■ PREPAYMENT CONVENTIONS

Borrowers can return principal early by prepaying their loans fully or in part. Measuring the prepayments from an entire pool, which is a collection of loans, could be done by actually tabulating the prepaid dollars. This would be an accurate measure but an unwieldy way to compare prepayments across different pools.

The market has settled on expressing prepayments relative to the dollar balance of the pool. Three measures are currently used to report prepayment rates, shown in Table 3-1. Each measure has usefulness depending upon the type of security and context of the need to measure and compare rates.

Table 3-1
Prepayment Conventions

Single Monthly Mortality (SMM)	The SMM measures the percentage of dollars prepaid in any month, expressed as a percentage of the expected mortgage balance.
Conditional Prepayment Rate (CPR)	CPR reflects the percentage prepayment rate resulting from converting the SMM to an annual rate. The CPR is best understood as the percentage of the nonamortized balance prepaid on an annual basis.
Public Securities Association Model (PSA)	An industry convention adopted by the Public Securities Association in which prepayment rates, expressed in CPR, are assumed to follow a standard path over time. This path assumes that the prepayment rate for a pool of loans increases gradually over the first 30 months and then levels out at a constant rate. Along the 100% PSA curve, the prepayment rate starts at 0.2% CPR in the first month and then rises 0.2% CPR per month until month 30 when the prepayment rate levels out at 6% CPR.

In order to develop a familiarity with the conventions, we will present a few equations and then work through some numerical examples.

Equation 3-1
Single Monthly[1] Mortality (SMM)

$$\text{SMM} = 100 \times \frac{(\text{Scheduled Balance} - \text{Actual Balance})}{\text{Scheduled Balance}}$$

In Equation 3-1, the scheduled balance represents the expected balance based upon normal amortization.

Equation 3-2
Conditional Prepayment Rate (CPR)

$$\text{CPR} = 100 \times \left(1 - \left(1 - \frac{\text{SMM}}{100}\right)^{12}\right)$$

Equation 3-3
Public Securities Association Prepayment Model (PSA)

$$\text{PSA} = 100 \times \frac{\text{CPR}}{\text{minimum(age, 30)} \times 0.2}$$

Using the above equations, we can develop some examples of calibrating prepayment rates.

[1]A variant of the formula for calculating SMM, CPR, and PSA can be found in the PSA Standard Formulas manual. Many of the other formulas in this chapter can also be found there.

Calculating Prepayment Rates[2]

Using information about the scheduled balance, actual balance and age, we can calculate the prepayment rates in SMM, CPR, and PSA formats as seen below.

Table 3-2

Sample Prepayment Rate Calculations

Scheduled balance	154,000.00
Actual balance	153,000.00
Age (months)	25
SMM	0.65%
CPR	7.53%
PSA	150.54%

Exercise 3-1

Given an MBS with an age of three and a CPR of 1%, what is the equivalent PSA rate ?

Exercise 3-2

Now repeat the exercise for the following pairs of ages and CPRs. The first month has already been calculated.

Work area

CPR	Age	PSA
1	1	500
1	2	
1	3	
1	4	
1	5	
6	30	
12	60	

[2]SMM, CPR, and PSA all represent percentages. It is common, however, for the % sign to be dropped and to refer, for example, to 200% PSA simply as 200 PSA.

Exercise 3-3

Convert PSA rates to CPR.

Work area

PSA	Age	CPR
100	1	
500	1	
1000	1	
1666	30	
200	2	

Exercise 3-4

Convert SMM to CPR and PSA equivalents.

Work area

Age	SMM	CPR	PSA
5	0.6		
6	1.0		
7	2.0		

■ CASHFLOWS

Mortgage payments made by fixed-rate borrowers have two interesting features: constant amounts and payment in arrears. A standard mortgage loan has a feature which allows the borrower to make a level payment each month. Part of this payment is allocated to interest and the remainder is used to pay down the principal. Initially the amount paid to interest greatly exceeds the amount allocated to principal. Over time this relationship changes and the allocation to principal increases greatly. The amount of the monthly cashflow is determined by using an annuity formula.

Payment in arrears means that the borrower makes the first payment one month after the loan is taken out. That is, a borrower who receives his loan on the first day of September makes the first payment on October 1. The interest amount will be based on the balance as of September 1.

To determine the monthly cashflow we use equation 3-4:

$$\text{Payment} = \frac{\text{Balance} \times \text{Coupon}/1200}{1 - (1 + \text{Coupon}/1200)^{-\text{Remaining term in months}}}$$

Equation 3-4
Monthly Payment for a Fixed-Rate Level Payment Loan

Coupon would be stated in annual terms. Use 8 for an 8% annual rate.

Determining the Monthly Payment

Table 3-3 shows an example of the monthly payment for a 9% mortgage with a balance of $200,000.

Table 3-3
Mortgage Characteristics

Balance	200,000.00
Coupon	9.00
Term (months)	360
Payment	1,609.25

Exercise 3-5

What is the monthly payment required for a 30-year 8.5% mortgage having an original balance of $150,000 ?

Exercise 3-6

Fill in the following matrix showing ranges of coupon and original balance. Assume a 30-year mortgage and solve for the constant monthly payment using Equation 3-4. A few cells have already been calculated.

Work area

			Balance		
Coupon	**$50,000**	**$100,000**	**$150,000**	**$200,000**	**$250,000**
4%	238.71				
6%					
8%	366.88				
10%					
12%					
14%					

By examining the matrix, we can see a way to judge the relative importance of coupon and balance. For a $50,000 loan, the improvement to the borrower when rates drop 200 basis points is on the order of $67 per month but for a $250,000 loan the improvement is closer to $335 per month.

Seeing the changes in cashflow as they vary by balance may shed a little light on the general differences between prepayment rates on GNMAs versus FNMA/FHLMC MBS. Generally we observe GNMA MBS to have lower prepayment rates than conventionals. This could be attributed to the majority of GNMA borrowers who have less financial means than the conventional borrowers. However, it may be more likely that the GNMAs, with their lower loan balances, may provide less of an absolute incentive to refinance than the higher balance conventionals.

■ BALANCE

After we know how to determine the monthly cashflows, there is another formula we could use to calculate the remaining balance of a loan. This formula will prove useful when calculating the scheduled balances that serve as input to the SMM formulas.

To determine the percent of the original balance for a given month (t) apply the following equation:

Equation 3-5
Percentage of Principal Balance Outstanding

$$\%\ \text{Balance}_t = 1 - \frac{(1 + \text{Coupon}/1200)^{\text{Age}} - 1}{(1 + \text{Coupon}/1200)^{\text{Original Term}} - 1}$$

In this equation, the age and original term are expressed in months. The coupon would be expressed as a whole number, for instance, 9. Age indicates the number of months the loan has existed. Without any partial prepayments, age plus remaining term equals the original term.

Calculating the Scheduled Balance

Table 3-4
Example of the Percent of Original Balance Calculation

Original Term	360
Age	40
Coupon	8.50
Percent of Original Balance	97.21%

If our original balance had been $150,000 the scheduled balance at the end of month 40 would be $145,815.

Exercise 3-7

What would be the percentage of original balance outstanding at the end of month 5 for a 30-year loan with a coupon of 9%?

Exercise 3-8

Compute the percentage of original balance outstanding for the following loans having the indicated coupons and ages. Assume that the original term is 360 months. The first cell has already been calculated.

Work area

	Coupon		
Age	**6%**	**8%**	**10%**
60	93.05%		
120			
180			
240			
300			
359			

■ MONTHLY AMORTIZATION

Using the tools created with the monthly payments and balance formulas, we have the necessary building blocks to actually project the cashflows for a mortgage loan. Using these cashflows we can break the payment down between principal and interest. The amortization analysis can be taken one step further to incorporate prepayments.

From Equation 3-4 we can solve for the monthly loan payment of a mortgage. This payment can then be broken down into principal and interest as shown in Formula 3-6.

$$\text{Monthly Payment} = \frac{\text{Coupon}}{1200} \times \text{Starting Principal} + \text{Amortized Principal}$$

Equation 3-6
Monthly Principal and Interest

To solve for the amortized principal we could follow two methods. First we could plug, that is make amortized principal the difference between the monthly payment and the interest payment. Alternatively, we could project out the scheduled principal balances using Equation 3-5. The difference between balances in any month would equate to the amount of principal amortized.

Allocating Monthly Cashflow between Interest and Principal

Using the cashflow from Table 3-3, we can allocate the first month's payment between interest and principal, as shown in Table 3-5.

Table 3-5

Allocation of Monthly Payment between Interest and Principal

Balance	200,000.00
Coupon	9.00
Term (months)	360
Payment	1,609.25
Interest	1,500.00
Principal	109.25

Exercise 3-9

Assume a 30-year loan with an 8.5% coupon and starting balance of $200,000. Break down the monthly payment between interest and principal and fill in the missing cells of the table. In the exercise, you could solve for the balance in either of the two manners described above. That is, you could decrease the balance by subtracting out the amortized principal or you could use the scheduled balance formula. Try using both methods. The first month has already been filled in.

Work area

Month	Balance	Principal	Interest
0	200,000.00		
1	199,878.84	121.16	1,416.67
2			
3			
4			
5			
6			

Pools versus a Single Loan

It is at this point that the distinction between a single loan and a pool of loans has to be considered. Up to now, we have described the mortgage math as it applies to a single loan. A pool of loans works in a similar manner. Generally only loans with similar characteristics will be pooled together, therefore, one can think intuitively of a pool as one huge loan. While this analogy works most of the time, it breaks down with the inclusion of prepayments.

Consider a standard level-payment fixed-rate mortgage with a 30-year maturity. If this loan has "prepayments," either one of two things is happening. Either the borrower is paying a little extra principal each month (also called curtailments), or the loan has been completely paid off through refinancing or selling the home (or through default).

Now consider a pool of the same type of mortgages. What happens to the pool as people prepay? If there are curtailments, the average maturity of the pool will decrease, but the scheduled payment will remain the same. However, if the prepayments are due to refinancing, selling the home, or default, then the average maturity of the pool will not be affected. (To see this, think of the average of the following set: {30, 30, 30}. If one of the loans is totally prepaid, the average of {30, 30} is still 30.) What will change is the monthly scheduled payment. Partial prepayments are generally a very small portion of prepayments.

When working on a pool level, the pool characteristics are calculated as averages of the underlying mortgages, as described in Table 3-6. Thus the coupon becomes the "WAC" and the maturity becomes the "WAM." As individual mortgages in a pool prepay over time, the WAC and WAM will change, corresponding to the actual make-up of the pool.

Table 3-6
Weighted Average MBS Characteristics

Weighted Average Coupon (WAC)	The mean of the gross coupon of the underlying mortgages that collateralize a security, weighted by the corresponding principal balances.
Weighted Average Loan Age (WALA)	The mean of the age of the underlying mortgages that collateralize a security.
Weighted Average Maturity (WAM)	The mean of the remaining term of the underlying mortgages that collateralize a security.

Note: WAC, WALA, and WAM are all calculated based upon the current principal balance.

When there are partial prepayments, the WAM will shorten, as we discussed above. But the WALA will not change. Thus, WALA plus WAM does not always equal the original term of the mortgages.

Because pool-level data is not readily available, analytical models generally use the most current weighted-average characteristics. Forecasting into the future, one cannot know which loans will prepay, and so the convention is to assume that a pool's mortgages are made up of identical mortgages whose coupons and maturity equal the WAC and the WAM, and that prepayments are always in full. This means that, unlike for a single loan, the scheduled payment for a pool has to be recalculated at every period. Thus, while it might be convenient to think of a pool as a single loan, one must keep in mind that this does not always work.

Including Prepayments

Building on the knowledge of monthly amortization, we are now ready to incorporate prepayment rates. Normally prepayment rates are specified as either a PSA or CPR equivalent. When working back to the cashflow level, a translation will have to be made to turn assumed PSA or CPR into an SMM.

Recall from Equation 3-1 that we can measure the SMM by examining the difference between the scheduled and the actual balance. We can then modify the formula to solve for the actual balance at the end of the first month given a scheduled balance and an SMM. Restating Equation 3-1 in these terms would provide the following:

Equation 3-7
Applying SMM to Calculate Actual Balance for Month 1

$$\text{Actual Balance}_1 = \text{Scheduled Balance}_1 \times \left(1 - \frac{\text{SMM}_1}{100}\right)$$

Calculating the Actual Balance with Prepayment Rates

Let's return to the cashflow example set up in Table 3-5, however now we will apply a 1% SMM rate (corresponding to 11.36% CPR).

Table 3-7
Including Prepayments

Balance	200,000.00
Coupon	9.00
Term (months)	360
Payment	1,609.25
Interest	1,500.00
Principal	109.25
SMM	1.00%
Scheduled Balance	199,890.75
Actual Balance	197,891.84
Prepaid Principal	1,998.91

Equation 3-7 is somewhat restrictive because it only considers the first month. We can generalize Equation 3-7 to give the actual balance when the SMM is held constant, as seen in Equation 3-8.

$$\text{Actual Balance}_t = \text{Scheduled Balance}_t \times \left[1 - \frac{SMM}{100}\right]^t$$

Equation 3-8
Applying SMM to Calculate Actual Balance for Constant SMM

For any constant prepayment rate, we can determine the actual balance by only knowing the scheduled balance and age of the loan (represented by the subscript t). Equation 3-8 can be taken one step further, generalizing for the case when the SMM is not constant each month. This can be seen in Equation 3-9.

$$\text{Actual Balance}_t = \text{Scheduled Balance}_t \times \prod_{t=1}^{Age} \left(1 - \frac{SMM_t}{100}\right)$$

Equation 3-9
Applying SMM to Calculate Actual Balance for Non-constant SMM

The mathematical symbol Π means that we take the product of the terms starting from t=1 and proceeding until the actual age of the mortgage in order to find the cumulative prepayment amount. Equations 3-8 and 3-9 can be used to save computing time when examining the cashflow pattern of a mortgage in the case of prepayments. The scheduled balance vector must only be calculated once and then scaled depending upon the level of prepayments. A more expensive (based on computing time) approach would be to recompute the scheduled balance by re-amortizing the payments based upon the prepayments.

Exercise 3-10

Restate Equations 3-2 and 3-3 in the following manner:

Solve for SMM given the CPR.

Solve for the CPR given the PSA.

Exercise 3-11

Assume a 30-year loan with a 9% coupon and an initial starting balance of $150,000. Compute the scheduled balance and the actual balance based upon a SMM rate of 1%. The actual balance for the first month has already been computed.

Work area

Month	Scheduled Balance	Actual Balance
0	150,000.00	
1		148,418.89
2		
3		
4		
5		

Exercise 3-12

Assuming the same mortgage characteristics, compute the actual balances assuming a 10% CPR. The first month has again been computed.

Work area

Month	Scheduled Balance	Actual Balance
0	150,000.00	
1		148,607.54
2		
3		
4		
5		

The difference between scheduled and actual balances for any given month equals the prepaid principal. We could now add this additional term to our monthly amortization analysis. Monthly cashflows can now be broken down between interest, amortized principal, and prepaid principal.

For any month we would determine the normal interest and amortized principal using the standard equation. The SMM would then be used to translate the percentage prepayment rate into an absolute level, measured in terms of dollars.

Calculating Cashflows with Prepayment Rates

We can now tie various concepts together in the calculation of monthly cashflows. The example will consider an MBS with a remaining term of 360 months, coupon of 7.5%, prepayment rate of 150% PSA, and a starting balance of $200,000. Table 3-8 contains the cashflows for the first six months.

Table 3-8

Cashflows for a 7.5% MBS at 150% PSA

Month	Balance	Interest	Principal Amortized	Prepaid	PSA	CPR	SMM
0	200,000.00						
1	199,801.54	1,250.00	148.43	50.03	150	0.3	0.025
2	199,552.12	1,248.76	149.32	100.10	150	0.6	0.050
3	199,251.77	1,247.20	150.18	150.17	150	0.9	0.075
4	198,900.56	1,245.32	151.00	200.20	150	1.2	0.101
5	198,498.61	1,243.13	151.79	250.16	150	1.5	0.126
6	198,046.06	1,240.62	152.55	300.00	150	1.8	0.151

The key part of the example is the changing monthly cashflow. When prepayments occur, we must re-amortize the balance. For example, based on the standard terms of the loan above, we would have a monthly cashflow of $1,398.43. This in fact corresponds to the sum of the amortized principal and interest for the first month. However, after the first prepayment we must determine the new level at which to reset the monthly cashflows. That is, we must calculate the monthly payment to fully amortize a loan of $199,801.54 with 359 months of remaining term. This turns out to be $1,398.08 (which again equals the interest and amortized principal for the second month). There are shortcuts to repeatedly using the amortization formula to determine the monthly cashflow. For example, we can back into the principal paid by looking at the change in monthly balance.

Exercise 3-13

Determining the Monthly Cashflow

Using the same security characteristics as in Table 3-8, calculate the monthly cashflows. However, now assume a prepayment rate of 300% PSA. The cashflows for the first month have already been filled in.

Work area

Month	Balance	Interest	Principal Amortized	Prepaid	PSA	CPR	SMM
0	200,000.00						
1	199,751.37	1,250.00	148.43	100.20	300	0.6	0.05
2							
3							
4							
5							
6							

■ ARMS

Borrowers can choose between taking out a loan with a fixed interest rate or one with an adjustable rate. The coupon rates for adjustable-rate mortgages (ARMs) adjust off of some specified index, including one-year Treasury rates, LIBOR, and the Cost of Funds Index. The most common cost of funds index, the 11th district, represents the average interest rate paid by savings institutions in that district for their deposits.

Due to the coupon that adjusts according to an index, the cashflows for an ARM are not constant over time. Payments may rise and fall depending on the level of the index. Other features govern the amount by which the coupon paid by the borrower can change. The most common characteristics of ARMS can be found in Table 3-9.

To determine the coupon paid by the borrower, we sum the index plus the gross margin. For example, consider an ARM indexed to the constant maturity one-year Treasury bill (usually termed one-year CMT) that had a gross margin of 175 basis points. If the one-year T-bill rate were 6.1%, the borrower would pay a coupon of 7.85%. If the servicing and guarantee fee summed to 65 basis points, the net margin paid to the investor would be 110 basis points.

The periodic collars define the maximum range that the borrower's coupon can move at the reset date. If we go back to our previous example and assume a 1% periodic rate cap, then the coupon could rise to 8.85% or fall to 6.65%. Smaller periodic caps work in the favor of the borrower when interest rates are rising.

Lifetime caps and floors denote the maximum or minimum coupon that a borrower could pay. Based upon the previous example, and assuming the maximum lifetime coupon is 500 basis points above the initial coupon, the highest rate a borrower could pay would be 12.85%.

Table 3-9
ARM Characteristics

Index Value	The ARM coupon will be based upon a market index. The most common index is the 1-year Treasury rate.
Initial Coupon	The initial gross coupon reflects the rate paid by the borrower until the first reset date. Because of competitive market pressures ARMs are sometimes originated with a below-market "teaser rate."
Gross Margin	The spread over the index paid by the borrower. This spread includes both servicing and guarantee fees or credit enhancement. The guarantee fee only exists for loans insured by a Government Sponsored Enterprise (GSE), such as FNMA or FHLMC and government agencies.
Net Margin	The spread paid to the investor after deducting the servicing and guarantee fees or credit enhancement.
Reset Frequency	Standard amount of time between coupon resets. Some ARMs have a monthly reset, but most Treasury ARMs reset on an annual basis. On the other hand, an ARM indexed to COFI could have the coupon reset each month.
Periodic Rate Collar	The maximum amount at which the coupon paid by the borrowers is allowed to change at each reset. Typical conventional 1-year Treasury ARMs have a 2% annual rate collar, GNMAs have a 1% periodic rate collar.
Gross Life Cap	The highest potential interest rate paid by the borrower. In most cases the gross life cap would be between 500 and 600 basis points above the initial coupon.
Gross Life Floor	Lowest potential interest rate paid by the borrower.

Depending upon competitive pressures, some originators of ARMs may give borrowers a loan with a below market initial coupon. These coupons are termed "teaser rates" as they act as an incentive for a borrower to choose an adjustable rate over a fixed-rate mortgage contract. For example, although the fully indexed rate may be 7.85%, an originator may set the coupon at 5% for the first 6 or 12 months. Because lifetime caps are generally set as a spread to the initial coupon, teaser rate ARMS may provide an additional benefit to the borrower of a low lifetime cap.

ARM Resets

Assume that a borrower takes out a new ARM loan with terms specified in Table 3-10. Assuming that the current one-year CMT was 5.5%, the fully indexed rate would be 7.5% (5.5 + 2.0). The investor, however, would only receive 3.35% (4.0 – 0.65), during the first payment period because of the teaser rate of 4%. The fully indexed net coupon that the investor would receive if there hadn't been a teaser rate is 6.85 (7.5 – 0.65).

Table 3-10
Sample ARM Terms

Feature	Rate
Index Value	One-year Constant Maturity Treasury (CMT)
Initial Coupon	4%
Gross Margin	200 basis points
Servicing	65 basis points
Reset Frequency	12 months
Periodic Collar	2%
Lifetime Cap	10%

Let's assume that, at the first reset, the one-year CMT rate remained constant at 5.5%. At this point, the coupon paid by the borrower would be reset to 6%. Although the fully indexed rate would still be 7.5%, the adjustment is restricted by the periodic collar of 2%.

Exercise 3-14

Assume an ARM with a gross margin of 175 basis points, 65 basis points of servicing/guarantee fees, an initial coupon of 5.1%, periodic cap of 1%. What will the coupon reset to at the following dates, assuming the listed one-year CMT rates? The reset for the first year has already been calculated.

Work area

		Coupon	
Year	**1-Year CMT**	**Gross**	**Net**
0		5.10	4.45
1	8.20	6.10	5.45
2	5.00		
3	5.75		
4	4.00		

■ MARKET CONVENTIONS

Loan and pooling factors add further complications to MBS. In particular, investors need to consider the effects of delay, accrued interest, and delivery variance when analyzing investment opportunities and in designing trading/settlement systems. Special pricing conventions may also confuse the newcomer.

Price Conventions

MBS prices are usually quoted as a percentage of the face value of the bond and in 32nds. For example, if a price was quoted of 102-10, that would be equivalent to 102 and 10/32. Converted into decimal, 102-10 would equal 102.313%. To calculate the actual dollar amount that would be paid, multiply 1.02313 times the balance or face value of the bond.

In the bond market, a 32nd is commonly called a "tick." A half of a 32nd (or 64th) is called a plus and is denoted by a + sign. For example, 102-10+ equals 102.328 in decimal. A "par" bond means the bond is selling at a price of 100. A price below 100 is termed a "discount" while a price above 100 is selling at a "premium."

Delay

Mortgage borrowers make their payments in arrears, with payments normally due the first of the month (although payments can generally be received by the servicer later than the first without incurring any late charge.) The time between the due date of the loan payment and the cash payment made to the investor is called the delay.

Delay allows servicers time to process an enormous number of cashflows that do not all arrive on the first of the month. However, the delay also gives the various intermediaries an opportunity to earn float income on the cash waiting to be disbursed to the investors, while investors lose potential income. Since timing is an important factor in present value, delay is accounted for by the investors in the price paid for an MBS.

Costs of Delay

Assuming that the current risk free interest rate is 6.25% (quoted on an actual/actual basis), each day of delay costs $171.23 for an investor expecting a $1 million cashflow.

Exercise 3-15

Calculating the Cost of Delay

Assume that an investor is expecting a $1 million cashflow that has been delayed for 15 days and the current risk free interest rate is 6.50% (actual/actual). What is the total opportunity cost to the investor of having the payment delayed?

Accrued Interest

The accrual of interest is essentially a zero-sum issue for the investor. At the time of settlement the investor must pay the seller interest earned on the investment from the beginning of the month to the settlement date. In return, the investor is entitled to the entire monthly coupon. There is a subtle twist, though: the seller receives his accrued interest rate payment as of the settlement date, while the investor can only get his payment on a delayed basis.

Interest accrues starting from the first of the month and assumes that MBS pay interest on a 30/360 basis. Each month is assumed to have 30 days so the daily interest rate can be found as shown in Equation 3-10:

Equation 3-10
Daily Interest Rate

$$\text{Daily Coupon} = \frac{\text{Annual Coupon}}{360}$$

Exercise 3-16

Assuming settlement on the 15th, what would be the accrued interest on an 8.5% MBS with principal balance of $5 million?

Variance and Pools Per Million

Passthrough MBS trading occurs either on a pool specific basis or on a To-Be-Announced (TBA) basis. When trading specific pools, buyers and sellers agree on price and amount of original face value. The seller has no latitude regarding the delivery specifications.

However, in the TBA market, the Public Securities Association (PSA) sets standards regarding acceptable delivery rules. These trading practices are meant to facilitate trading. They also provide opportunities for incremental profits.

Based on current standards, the seller can modify the amount of principal delivered. The dollar variance between actual and expected delivery must be between plus or minus 1% of the original trade amount. Taking advantage of the variance rules based upon market conditions is an accepted trading practice, and many dealers have designed sophisticated technology to use the variance to their advantage.

Exercise 3-17

A commercial bank agrees to sell a dealer $5mm of GNMA 9s on a TBA basis at a price of $103-16 and an allowed variance of 1%. At the settlement date the price of the GNMA 9s has increased to $104-00. Will the commercial bank deliver $5mm worth of GNMA 9s? If not, how much will they deliver?

With the continual maturation of the MBS market, many pools now trade with relatively small balances. Each pool requires clerical support for tracking and verifying principal and interest payments. Assuming a fixed cost per pool, many investors prefer to hold as few small pools as possible. To prevent sellers from dumping many small balance pools onto purchasers, the PSA has set guidelines regarding the maximum number of pools deliverable for TBA trades. These limits depend upon both the coupon of the security and the size of the trades. For coupons below 11%, a seller may deliver up to three pools per million dollars and for coupons 11% and above sellers can deliver five pools per million. There are additional limitations regarding tail pieces. For example, if two pools fall within the variance, a third small pool cannot be delivered.

■ ANALYSIS

The analysis section considers two aspects of MBS that are relevant in a static cashflow setting: yield and average life. In later chapters, the analysis will be extended to consider states of the environment when we do not specify a single interest rate scenario. The analysis tools developed in this section can be created in a spreadsheet application.

Yield

Yield is the standard measure of value for fixed-income securities. It presents a quick method to state the benefit of purchasing and holding a security until the final cashflow. In the context of finance, yield represents the internal rate of return assuming an initial purchase price and a stream of cash inflows.

In Equation 3-11 the subscript T represents the time after settlement (calibrated in months and including the actual delay days). The yield expressed in the formula above is called a mortgage equivalent yield as it assumes cash compounding occurring on a monthly basis. The price includes accrued interest.

The standard price and yield formula relationship can be seen in Equation 3-11:

Equation 3-11
Price and Yield for an MBS

$$\text{Price} = \frac{\text{Cash Flow}_{T_1}}{(1+\text{Yield}/1200)^{T_1}} + \ldots + \frac{\text{Cash Flow}_{T_{WAM}}}{(1+\text{Yield}/1200)^{T_{WAM}}}$$

$$\text{Price} = \sum_{i=1}^{WAM} \frac{\text{Cash Flow}_{T_i}}{(1+\text{Yield}/1200)^{T_i}}$$

Computing the Yield

Assume an annual coupon paying security with a coupon of 5% and a current price of $101 and two years until maturity. The cashflows and yield have been computed in Table 3-11.

Table 3-11
Sample Yield Calculation

Year	Cashflow
0	-101.00
1	5.00
2	105.00
Yield	4.00%

Exercise 3-18

Using the bond from Table 3-11, what would the yield be if the initial price were $99? (Hint: This is done easily using a spreadsheet and an IRR or goal seek function. IRR functions are also available on some calculators. If you are doing it by hand, you will need to use the quadratic formula or a trial and error approach.)

Standardizing Yield

The yield calculation shown in Equation 3-11 assumes that the MBS pays on a monthly basis. As a market convention, most yields are stated on a semi-annual basis which is called bond equivalent yield. That is, yields are quoted as if a security pays a coupon twice a year. In order to compare the yield calculated in Equation 3-11 to other securities, we must adjust the compounding basis from a monthly yield to a semi-annual equivalent. Intuitively, we're trying to solve the following question: What is the semi-annual coupon rate at which the investor is indifferent between receiving monthly or semi-annual payments?

This question can be expressed in the following formula (MEY represents the yield as quoted in monthly terms while BEY represents a yield quoted based on semi-annual compounding):

Equation 3-12
Monthly and Bond Equivalent Yields

$$(1+\frac{MEY}{1200})^{12} = (1+\frac{BEY}{200})^{2}$$

Solving for the BEY as a function of the MEY:

$$BEY = 200 \times \left((1+\frac{MEY}{1200})^{6} - 1 \right)$$

Exercise 3-19

Assuming that an MBS had a monthly equivalent yield of 8%, what would be the bond equivalent yield ?

Average Life

As a concept, maturity works well to describe the period that an investor in corporate or Treasury bonds keeps his principal outstanding. However, with MBS the maturity can be rather misleading. For a 30-year MBS, it is quite true that the final payment, or maturity, occurs with the 360th cashflow. However, the amortizing nature of the security provides a return of principal to the investor over the entire 30-year period.

In lieu of maturity, investors rely on the weighted average life (WAL) of the MBS as a proxy for maturity. The WAL indicates the average amount of time that $1 of principal remains outstanding. WAL can be calculated based on the following formula:

Equation 3-13
Weighted Average Life

$$\text{Average Life} = \frac{\sum_{i=1}^{WAM} T_i \times \text{Principal}_i}{\sum_{i=1}^{WAM} \text{Principal}_i}$$

In Equation 3-13 the variable T represents the time until the principal payment. This time dimension could be stated in months or days. Normally the WAL will be quoted in years, so the calculation must be adjusted to place the time into the proper units. The principal payments must also be adjusted for the delay.

Calculating Average Life

Assume a security that amortizes annually over five years, using the amortization schedule below the average life equals 3.5 years. The principal cashflows are shown in Table 3-12.

Table 3-12
Principal Cashflows

Time	Principal
1	10.00
2	15.00
3	20.00
4	25.00
5	30.00
Total Principal	100.00
WAL	3.50

Exercise 3-20

Given the amortization schedule in the table below compute the average life.

Work area

Time	Principal
1	5.00
2	10.00
3	20.00
4	40.00
5	80.00
Total Principal	155.00
WAL	

Cashflow Duration

Duration is a tricky issue in regard to MBS. Normally we think of duration as providing some measure for the time value weighting of cashflows. Duration can alternatively be used as a risk measure. In this case, duration would represent the price sensitivity to a change in interest rates. MBS market participants should be aware that duration can come in three basic varieties: Macaulay, modified, and effective.

Macaulay Duration

The Macaulay duration represents a time-weighted value of cashflows. For a security whose cashflows do not change with interest rates, the Macaulay duration can be shown to equal the percentage change in price for a percentage change in yield.

Equation 3-14
Macaulay Duration

$$\text{Duration} = \frac{1}{\text{Price}} \times \left(\sum_{i=1}^{WAM} \frac{T_i \times \text{Cashflow}}{(1 + \text{yield}/200)^{2Ti}} \right)$$

Where:

T = the time elapsed from settlement until receipt of cashflows

Yield = bond equivalent yield

Table 3-13 computes the Macaulay duration for a 2-year, semi-annual 6% coupon-bearing security, currently priced at $100 having a yield of 6%.

Table 3-13
Sample Macaulay Duration Calculation

Time	Cashflow	Time Weighted Discounted Cashflow
0.5	3.00	1.4563
1.0	3.00	2.8278
1.5	3.00	4.1181
2.0	103.00	183.0283
Yield	6.00	
Price	100.00	
Duration	1.91	

The third column in the table represents the term that is summed in Equation 3-14. This term has been labeled the time-weighted discounted cashflow.

Modified Duration

The modified duration makes a slight change in the Macaulay duration formula. It represents the percentage change in price for a basis point change in yield, rather than a percentage change in yield.

Equation 3-15
Modified Duration

$$\text{Modified Duration} = \frac{\text{Duration}}{1+\dfrac{\text{Yield}}{200}}$$

Exercise 3-21

Convert the Macaulay duration from Table 3-10 to a modified duration.

Effective Modified Duration

For a security like an MBS, measures of modified and Macaulay duration have little meaning when it comes to interest rate risk management. Both modified and Macaulay duration do not take into account the effect changes in interest rates have on MBS cashflows through prepayments. This cashflow sensitivity of MBS leads us to use an empirical calculation for duration shown in Equation 3-16, below.

The prices in the shifted scenarios will reflect changing prepayments and pricing assumptions. These prices can be estimated by either using a valuation model, such as OAS, or by determining an approximate change in the prepayment rates and spread of an MBS to an appropriate Treasury benchmark based on the shift in the yield curve.

Equation 3-16
Effective Modified Duration

$$\text{Effective Modified Duration} = \frac{-100}{\text{Price}_{\text{Base}}} \times \frac{\text{Price}_{+\Delta\text{Yield Scenario}} - \text{Price}_{-\Delta\text{Yield Scenario}}}{2 \times \Delta\text{Yield}}$$

Issues related to the effective duration will be explored further in Chapter 7.

Exercise 3-22 (Advanced)

Create a graph with age on the x-axis and CPR on the y-axis. Make plots of the curves representing 50, 100, 200 and 500% PSA.

Exercise 3-23 (Advanced)

Based on the analysis in Exercise 3-8, compute the percentage of scheduled balances for the following table.

Work area

8% Coupon

Age	180-Month Original Term	360-Month Original Term
24		
48		
72		
96		
120		
144		
168		

Should the scheduled balance for the 360-month original term loan always be twice the amount as the scheduled balance for the 180-month loan?

Exercise 3-24 (Advanced)

Assume a newly created 30-year, 8% MBS. Break down payments over the first six months between interest, amortized principal, and prepayments. First, assume a prepayment rate of 7% CPR. In the second case, assume that prepayments will occur according to 300% of the PSA model. Using a spreadsheet, extend the results to the maturity of the MBS.

Work area

7% CPR

	Monthly	Actual		Principal	
Month	CPR	Balance	Interest	Scheduled	Prepaid
0		150,000.00			
1	7%				
2	7%				
3	7%				
4	7%				
5	7%				
6	7%				

300% PSA

	Monthly	Actual		Principal	
Month	CPR	Balance	Interest	Scheduled	Prepaid
0		150,000.00			
1					
2					
3					
4					
5					
6					

■ REVIEW QUESTIONS

Why do borrowers choose ARMs instead of fixed-rate loans? What might the implications be regarding expected prepayment effects?

Is it more reasonable to determine the effect of delay by using the risk-free rate or by assuming another discounting rate?

Why should the bond equivalent yield be higher than the monthly equivalent yield? Why is CPR less than 12 times the SMM?

ANSWERS TO EXERCISES

3-1

$$\text{PSA} = 100 \times \frac{1}{\text{minimum}(3,\ 30) \times 0.2}$$

$$\begin{aligned}\text{PSA} &= 100 \times \frac{1}{3 \times 0.2} \\ &= 166.67\end{aligned}$$

3-2

CPR	Age	PSA
1	1	500
1	2	250
1	3	167
1	4	125
1	5	100
6	30	100
12	60	200

3-3

PSA	Age	CPR
100	1	0.20
500	1	1.00
1,000	1	2.00
1,666	30	99.96
200	2	0.80

3-4

Age	SMM	CPR	PSA
5	0.6	6.97	697
6	1.0	11.36	947
7	2.0	21.53	1,538

3-5

Monthly payment is $1,153.37.

3-6

			Balance		
Coupon	$50,000	$100,000	$150,000	$200,000	$250,000
4%	238.71	477.42	716.12	954.83	1,193.54
6%	299.78	599.55	899.33	1,199.10	1,498.88
8%	366.88	733.76	1,100.65	1,467.53	1,834.41
10%	438.79	877.57	1,316.36	1,755.14	2,193.93
12%	514.31	1,028.61	1,542.92	2,057.23	2,571.53
14%	592.44	1,184.87	1,777.31	2,369.74	2,962.18

3-7

Percentage of original balance outstanding is 99.7228%.

3-8

Age	6%	Coupon 8%	10%
60	93.05%	95.07%	96.57%
120	83.69%	87.72%	90.94%
180	71.05%	76.78%	81.66%
240	54.00%	60.48%	66.41%
300	31.01%	36.19%	41.30%
359	0.60%	0.73%	0.87%

3-9

Month	Balance	Principal	Interest
0	200,000.00		
1	199,878.84	121.16	1,416.67
2	199,756.82	122.02	1,415.81
3	199,633.94	122.88	1,414.94
4	199,510.19	123.75	1,414.07
5	199,385.56	124.63	1,413.20
6	199,260.04	125.51	1,412.31

3-10

$$SMM = 100 \times \left(1 - \left(1 - \frac{CPR}{100}\right)^{\frac{1}{12}}\right)$$

$$CPR = \frac{PSA \times \min(\text{age},\ 30) \times 0.2}{100}$$

3-11

Month	Scheduled Balance	Actual Balance
0	150,000.00	
1	149,918.07	148,418.89
2	149,835.52	146,853.79
3	149,752.35	145,304.56
4	149,668.56	143,771.02
5	149,584.14	142,253.03

3-12

Month	Scheduled Balance	Actual Balance
0	150,000.00	
1	149,918.07	148,607.54
2	149,835.52	147,227.36
3	149,752.35	145,859.35
4	149,668.56	144,503.40
5	149,584.14	143,159.42

3-13

			Principal				
Month	Balance	Interest	Amortized	Prepaid	PSA	CPR	SMM
0	200,000.00						
1	199,751.37	1,250.00	148.43	100.20	300	0.6	0.050
2	199,401.38	1,248.45	149.28	200.71	300	1.2	0.101
3	198,949.94	1,246.26	150.06	301.37	300	1.8	0.151
4	198,397.13	1,243.44	150.77	402.04	300	2.4	0.202
5	197,743.16	1,239.98	151.41	502.56	300	3.0	0.254
6	196,988.40	1,235.89	151.97	602.79	300	3.6	0.305

3-14

Year	CMT1	Coupon Gross	Coupon Net
0		5.10	4.45
1	8.20	6.10	5.45
2	5.00	6.75	6.10
3	5.75	7.50	6.85
4	4.00	6.50	5.85

3-15

Delay cost is $2,671.23.

3-16

Accrued interest is $16,527.78. (Note: Settlement is on the 15th, so there are 14 accrual days.)

3-17

The bank will not deliver $5 million; it will deliver $4.95 million.

3-18

The yield is 6%.

3-19

The bond equivalent yield is 8.1345%.

3-20

The WAL is 4.16129 years.

3-21

The modified duration is 1.85.

3-22

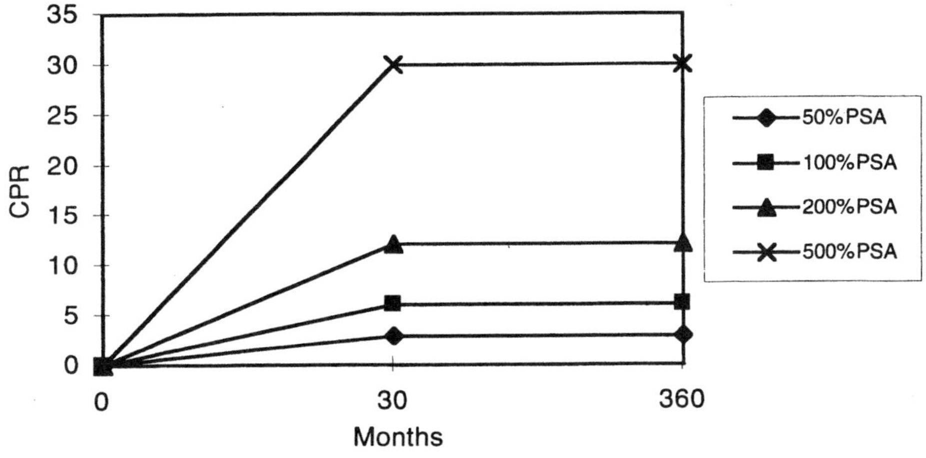

3-23

8% Coupon

Age	180-Month Original Term	360-Month Original Term
24	92.51%	98.26%
48	83.72	96.22
72	73.41	93.83
96	61.31	91.02
120	47.13	87.72
144	30.50	83.86
168	10.99	79.33

No, the scheduled balance for a 360 term loan is not twice the amount of a 180-month loan.

3-24

7% CPR

Month	Monthly CPR	Actual Balance	Interest	Principal Scheduled	Principal Prepaid
0		150,000.00			
1	7	148,995.56	1,000.00	100.65	903.79
2	7	147,997.12	993.30	100.71	897.73
3	7	147,004.64	986.65	100.77	891.71
4	7	146,018.09	980.03	100.83	885.73
5	7	145,037.42	973.45	100.89	879.78
6	7	144,062.61	966.92	100.95	873.87

300% PSA

Month	Monthly CPR	Actual Balance	Interest	Principal Scheduled	Principal Prepaid
0		150,000.00			
1	0.6	149,824.20	1,000.00	100.65	75.16
2	1.2	149,572.38	998.83	101.27	150.55
3	1.8	149,244.46	997.15	101.84	226.08
4	2.4	148,840.48	994.96	102.36	301.62
5	3.0	148,360.59	992.27	102.84	377.06
6	3.6	147,805.04	989.07	103.26	452.28

CHAPTER FOUR

Environmental Alternatives

Now that Susan was moving into more complicated aspects of the MBS market, new terms kept on cropping up. The research reports were constantly referring to things like forward rates, term structures of volatility, par curves, and interest rate trees. Susan had a basic grasp of these financial terms from her MBA training and CFA study courses, but her favorite salesman told Susan that he did not believe in forward rates. Susan was at a loss. There seemed to be another world going on below the surface of the analysis. Now was the time to get a cup of latté and become an honorary member of the rocket science club.

INTRODUCTION

While there are many factors that influence the behavior of mortgage-backed securities (MBS), the largest environmental factor is the level of interest rates. Interest rates play an important role in determining mortgage prepayments because the level of interest rates relative to a homeowner's mortgage rate creates the incentive to refinance. For MBS valuation, the rate at which cashflows are discounted is determined by a yield curve, usually the Treasury. Because future cashflows are uncertain, the level of interest rate volatility is crucial for building probable interest rate scenarios. Of course, there are many other variables that should be considered in MBS valuation such as housing market activity and overall economic growth but we will not discuss them here. For ease of calculation, in this chapter interest rates are often expressed in decimal form. For example, 5% equals 0.05.

FORWARD RATES

Forward rates can be thought of as the market's assessment of how it values future cashflows. MBS are virtually always priced from models that make forward rate assumptions. The calculation of forward rates from existing spot rates is a simple exercise.

Suppose you have to choose between two investments, A and B. Investment A is a two-year zero-coupon bond with a yield of 7.0%. Investment B is a series of two one-year zero-coupon bonds, the second bond bought after the first bond matures. The first one-year bond has a yield of 5%. The one-year forward rate would be the yield on the second bond, which makes the investor indifferent between the two investment strategies.

Using standard compounding math, we can find the return from the two investment strategies. The return on $1 investment in strategy A is $(1+.07)^2$, whereas the return on investment B is $(1+.05) \times (1+ {}_1F_1)$, where ${}_1F_1$ is the forward rate for a one-year zero-coupon bond, one year from now. For the investor to be indifferent, the return on these two investments should be equal. Using algebra, one can solve for ${}_1F_1$:

Equation 4-1
Solving for ${}_1F_1$, One-Year Forward Rate

$$(1+.07)^2 = (1+.05) \times (1+ {}_1F_1)$$
$${}_1F_1 = 0.0904$$
$${}_1F_1 = 9.04\%$$

This methodology can be used to find forward rates for any maturity for any year in the future, given the appropriate rates. For example, if a zero-coupon bond with a maturity of three years yields 7.5%, we can then use the above yields to find the forward rate for a two-year bond, one year hence, and a one-year bond, two years hence, as shown below:

Finding the forward rate for a two-year bond, one year forward:

$$(1+.075)^3 = (1+.05) \times (1+{}_1F_2)^2$$
$${}_1F_2 = 0.0877$$
$${}_1F_2 = 8.77\%$$

Finding the forward rate for a one-year bond, two years forward:

$$(1+.075)^3 = (1+.07)^2 \times (1+{}_2F_1)$$
$${}_2F_1 = 0.0851$$
$${}_2F_1 = 8.51\%$$

Given an entire spot-rate yield curve that is the graph of interest rates as a function of time, one can find a forward yield curve for each year in the future.

■ STRIPPING THE PAR-YIELD CURVE

Notice that in the above discussion, the bonds were specified to be 'zero coupon.' This means that no coupon is paid out during the life of the bond. A lump sum of money is paid out on the maturity date. The absence of a coupon allows us to use the simple compounding formula in Equation 4-1 to derive the forward rates. If coupons are paid, then the computation is not as straightforward since one must take into account the reinvestment of the coupon payments. To avoid confusion, for the rest of this discussion, we will refer to the current yield curve associated with zero-coupon bonds as the spot curve and the individual zero-coupon yields as the spot rate. The common names for the different yield curves are shown in Table 4-1.

Table 4-1

Yield Curve Terminology

Spot Curve	The yield curve associated with bonds that do not pay any coupon during the life of the bond. Instead, zero-coupon bonds are traded at a discount (i.e. at a price less than face value). The spot curve rates can be taken from actual bonds being actively traded as well as artificially derived from stripping the par-yield curve.
Par-Yield Curve	The yield curve associated with bonds that pay coupon periodically and that are priced at par (i.e. at 100% of the face value).
Forward Curve	The implicit curves that show the market's assessment of how it will value future cashflows. There is a forward yield curve for every period in the future. These curves can be derived from the spot and the par-yield curves. The forward curves can be expressed as either par-yields or spot rates.

In order to find forward rates associated with coupon paying bonds of different maturities, trading at par (termed the par-yield curve), one can use the following methodology:

1. Strip the par-yield curve to get the spot curve.
2. Use the spot curve to get the forward-spot curve.
3. Reconstitute the forward-spot curve to get the forward par-yield curve.

The "bootstrapping" method is used to strip the par-yield curve. Each coupon-bearing bond, if discounted at the appropriate spot rate, will be valued at par, or 100. That is the definition of the par-yield curve. Thus, if we know the first spot rate and the par-yield curve, we can solve for all the spot rates.

To derive the spot curve, we start with the bond whose maturity equals one period. The yield of this bond will be the first one-period spot rate.

The next spot rate can be found using the two-period par bond. Discount the first set of cashflows with the one-period spot rate. The second set of cashflows should be discounted by the two-period spot rate, which is unknown. However, we can solve for the two-period spot rate because by definition, the sum of the discounted cashflows equals 100. By extension, the third-period spot rate may be found using the third-period par bond, and so on.

For example, assume the par yield curve in Table 4-2 where each bond pays out an annual coupon:

Table 4-2
A Sample Par-Yield Curve

Year	1	2	3	4
Yield	5.0	6.5	8.0	9.0

The first spot rate (S_1) will simply be 5.0% because the interest will only be paid at the maturity date of one year. The next bond pays 6.5% interest every year for two years. The first year's cashflow, given a bond with a principal amount of $100, will be $6.50. In the second year, the cashflow includes both the $6.50 interest payment plus the principal of $100. To find the next spot rate, S_2, solve the following equation for S_2, where rates are in decimal (i.e. 0.05).

$$100 = \frac{CF_1}{(1+S_1)} + \frac{CF_2}{(1+S_2)^2}$$

$$100 = \frac{6.5}{(1+.05)} + \frac{106.5}{(1+S_2)^2}$$

$$(1+S_2)^2 = \frac{106.5}{100 - \frac{6.5}{(1+.05)}}$$

$$S_2 = \sqrt{\frac{106.5}{100 - \frac{6.5}{(1+.05)}}} - 1$$

$$S_2 = 0.06549$$

$$S_2 = 6.549\%$$

To reconstitute a spot curve into a par-yield curve, just do the above calculation in reverse. That is, instead of solving for the spot rates, solve for the interest cashflow that, when discounted at the spot rates, will equal par. Equation 4-2 shows the generic equation for either stripping the par-yield curve or reconstituting the spot curve. It is simply the price-yield equation described in Chapter 3 (Equation 3-11), with the price set equal to par.

$$100 = \frac{CF_1}{(1+S_1)^1} + \frac{CF_2}{(1+S_2)^2} + \frac{CF_3}{(1+S_3)^3} + \ldots \frac{CF_n}{(1+S_n)^n}$$

Equation 4-2
Solve for S_n to Strip or CF_n to Reconstitute the Curve

Exercise 4-1

Given the par coupon yield curve below, strip the curve to find the spot curve, then calculate all the implied spot forward rates.

Year	1	2	3	4
Yield	7.0	8.0	9.0	10.0

Hint: You can calculate six forward rates.

Work area

Year of Maturity	1	2	3	4
Spot Curve				

	Year Forward		
Maturity	**1**	**2**	**3**
1			
2			
3			

Exercise 4-2

Determine the forward rates from the following spot curve. Then determine the par-yield curve from the spot rates and the forward par-yield curve from the forward spot rates.

Year	1	2	3	4
Yield	10.0	9.0	8.0	7.0

Work area

Maturity	**1**	**2**	**3**	**4**
Spot Curve	10.0	9.00	8.00	7.00
Par Curve				

Forward spot rates:

		Year Forward	
Maturity	**1**	**2**	**3**
1			
2			
3			

Forward par rates:

		Year Forward	
Maturity	**1**	**2**	**3**
1			
2			
3			

■ VOLATILITY OF INTEREST RATES

Because the future is unknown, MBS valuation requires some kind of projection of future interest rates. While the forward rates described in the previous section are the market's prediction of future interest rates, we would like to create a set of possible interest rate scenarios. In order to create interest rate scenarios, one must have some idea of what type of movements are plausible. Interest rate volatility is one measure to describe the way interest rates change. The volatility of interest rates refers to the standard deviation of yield movements. A standard deviation measures the extent of variation around the mean. Interest rate volatility is normally stated in terms of an annualized percentage. Yield volatility is an important input into option valuation models.

The Mean

To calculate the extent of variation around the mean, one must first find the sample mean, $\overline{x}$, or average of a set of n measurements, x_1, $x_2, \ldots, x_n$. This is expressed as:

Equation 4-3
The Sample Mean

$$\overline{x} = \frac{\sum_{i=1}^{n} x_i}{n}$$

The Variance and Standard Deviation

The variation of data points around the mean is reflected in the difference of each data point from the mean: $(x_i - \bar{x})$. These are called deviations. To find an overall indicator of deviation for the entire set of data points, we might want to take the average of these deviations. The average of the deviations, however, would equal zero. In order to obtain a non zero number, we can calculate the sample variance, s^2, which is an average of the squared deviations:

$$s^2 = \frac{\sum_{i=1}^{n}(x_i - \bar{x})^2}{n-1}$$

This can be calculated more easily as:

Equation 4-4
The Sample Variance

$$s^2 = \frac{\sum_{i=1}^{n} x_i^2 - n\bar{x}^2}{n-1}$$

The standard deviation, *s*, is simply the square root of the variance.

Calculating Yield Volatility

Given daily yield data, it is a simple exercise to calculate yield volatility for a particular maturity. The procedure is as follows given we have daily yields for a particular security, Y_i, where i = 1, 2,…n:

1. Calculate the relative yield change, Y_i/Y_{i-1} for each day.
2. Take the natural log of the daily relative change, $\ln(Y_i/Y_{i-1})$ for each day.
3. Calculate the standard deviation of the daily log relative changes.
4. The standard deviation of the daily log relative change is converted to an annual percentage basis by scaling the measure by the number of trading days in a year. This is usually approximated to be 250 (365 minus weekends and some holidays). To convert the daily standard deviation to the annual standard deviation, multiply by the square root of 250.

Equation 4-5
Finding Annual Standard Deviation

$$\text{Annual Standard Deviation} = \text{Daily Standard Deviation} \times \sqrt{\text{trading days per year}}$$

A two standard deviation range of interest rates represents a 95% confidence interval for interest rates. Thus, plotting the lower and upper ranges of possible interest rates within this 95% confidence interval can give a sense of the range of possible interest rate fluctuation.

Exercise 4-3

Given the tables below, calculate the yield volatility, expressed as an annual rate for one-year Treasuries and 30-year Treasuries. Then find the standard deviation measure stated in basis points. Does volatility change with maturity?

Constant Maturity 1-Year Treasury Bill Yields

Date	Yield	Date	Yield
2/13/95	6.82	2/20/95	6.60
2/14/95	6.73	2/21/95	6.65
2/15/95	6.64	2/22/95	6.46
2/16/95	6.57	2/23/95	6.50
2/17/95	6.61	2/24/95	6.47

30-Year Treasury Bill Yields

Date	Yield	Date	Yield
2/13/95	7.67	2/20/95	7.59
2/14/95	7.61	2/21/95	7.61
2/15/95	7.56	2/22/95	7.54
2/16/95	7.57	2/23/95	7.55
2/17/95	7.59	2/24/95	7.53

Work area

One-Year Volatility:

Date	Yield	Y_i/Y_{i-1}	$\ln(Y_i/Y_{i-1})$
2/13/95			
2/14/95			
2/15/95			
2/16/95			
2/17/95			
2/20/95			
2/21/95			
2/22/95			
2/23/95			
2/24/95			
Average			
Variance			
Daily Stan Dev			
Annual			
SD in BP			

30-Year Volatility:

Date	Yield	Y_i/Y_{i-1}	$\ln(Y_i/Y_{i-1})$
2/13/95			
2/14/95			
2/15/95			
2/16/95			
2/17/95			
2/20/95			
2/21/95			
2/22/95			
2/23/95			
2/24/95			
Average			
Variance			
Daily Stan Dev			
Annual			
SD in BP			

■ BINOMIAL TREES[1]

In the price-yield calculation from Chapter 3, interest rates are assumed to stay constant, which means mortgage cashflows are discounted with a single rate. In real life, interest rates are not constant over time. When cashflows are certain, discounting cashflows with today's yield curve is today's best valuation. But mortgage cashflows are not certain. In fact, they are highly dependent on interest rates through the prepayment option. Thus, one would like to know what will happen to our cashflows when interest rates change. There are many methods for modeling future interest rates. Here we discuss the binomial tree. We will build a tree of interest rates based upon the current yield curve and then use this tree to value bonds and options.

For bonds with embedded interest-rate dependent options, binomial models are the basic form of analysis. However for MBS, additional features are needed. These additional features will be discussed in Chapter 9. The models presented here are extremely simplified. In practice, there are a rich set of approaches to value these types of options.

A binomial tree takes the form shown in Figure 4-1. The first node, called the root, is simply the first period yield. The second level of nodes represents probable yields one period from now, while the third level of nodes represents probable rates two periods from now.

Figure 4-1
Binomial Tree

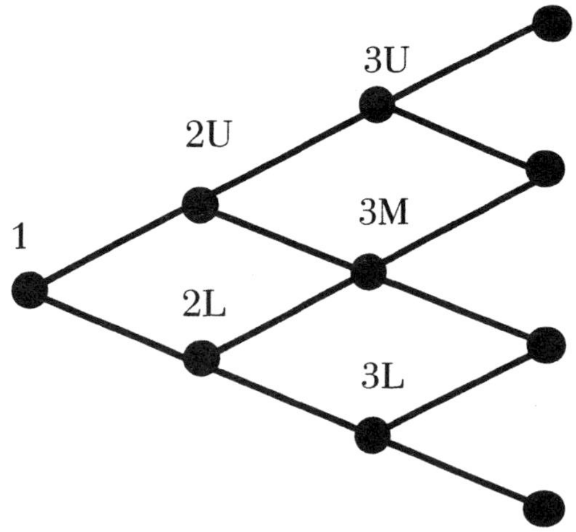

[1]All the binomial trees in this chapter were computer-generated using the *Yield Curve Primer* software, Andrew Kalotay Associates.

Each vertical set of nodes represents the rate possibilities for a time period in the future. A binomial tree using a discrete version of the log-normal process is characterized by three parameters:

1. A yield curve.
2. The relative probability of up and down moves.
3. Volatility.

We are assuming that the volatility is constant over all periods and that at each node, the probability of going up or down is equal. Thus, we will assume that the ratio between the upper and lower numbers in each of the nodes is e^{2V} where V is the short-term volatility in percentage per year, and e equals 2.718. The binomial tree must be consistent with the forward curve for no arbitrage. (This is a simplified explanation of the assumptions that go into a binomial tree. A complete treatment is beyond the scope of this chapter.)

The reasoning is as follows: at each node, one must determine the numbers such that (1) the proper ratio as described above holds true and (2) when a bond is valued using the binomial tree, the price will be equal to the current market price. Thus, an up branch to the right of any node represents an increase in yield, while a down branch is a decrease in yield, subject to the above two constraints.

Calculating a Sample Binomial Tree

Calculating a binomial tree involves numerical procedures. Unfortunately, the choice is between a trial and error approach or rather tedious closed-form solutions. The process for calculating a binomial tree is as follows. Consider the following par-yield curve in Table 4-3:

Table 4-3
A Sample Par-Yield Curve

Maturity	1	2	3
Par Yield	5.0	6.0	6.5

Assume that the annual volatility is 20%. Thus, the ratio between two nodes of the same level is $e^{0.40}$, which equals 1.49. The root is simply 5% or 0.05, as shown in Figure 4-2. To calculate the second level nodes, you first make a guess. A two-year bond would currently yield 6%, given the par-yield curve. The upper node should be a little higher and the lower node should be a little lower than 6%. If you make a guess for the lower node, simply multiply $e^{0.40}$ by your guess to get the upper node. If the two-year bond's cashflows are discounted by the correct tree, then the present value of the bond should equal 100, since that is the market's current valuation for the bond. (Remember, by definition, the par-yield curve is composed of bonds priced at 100, for different maturities.)

Figure 4-2
The Root of the Binomial Tree

Figure 4-3 shows the guesses for the second node. They are, in fact, the correct rates to show how the calculation should work. To demonstrate, take the two-year bond, whose cashflows are shown in Table 4-4:

Figure 4-3
Guesses for the Second Node of the Binomial Tree

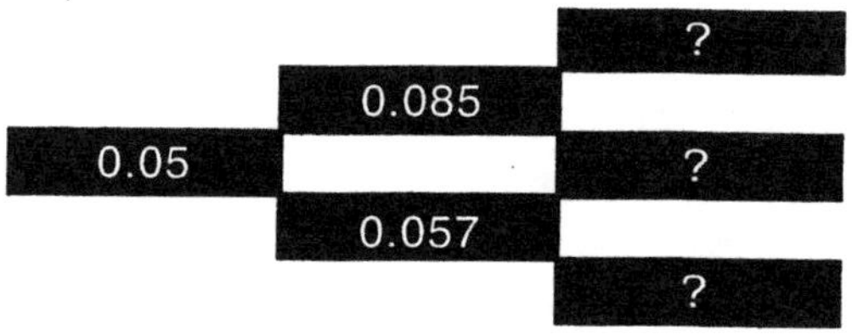

Table 4-4
Cashflows of Two-Year 6% Bond Priced at Par

Year	Cashflow
1	$6.00
2	$106.00

Table 4-5
Present Value of Two-Year 6% Bond from the Binomial Tree

Period	Lower	Upper
1	101.232	98.768
2	100.294	97.706

Steps to Calculate the Second Level[2]

1. Discount the \$106 by your guesses for the upper and lower nodes, 8.5% and 5.7%, respectively. (Notice that 5.7% × 1.49= 8.5%. This is shown in Figure 4-3 for the second period.) The discounted values shown in period two of Table 4-5 represent what the two-year bond would be worth one year from now.
2. If you add the first period cashflow, \$6, to the upper and lower values, you get \$106.294 and \$103.706.
3. Then, discounting these values by 5%, one gets the first period values shown in Table 4-5.
4. If you average these two values together, you get \$100: ((101.232 + 98.768)/2)=100. Alternatively, one could have averaged in Step 2 and then discounted the average by 5%. If one did not get \$100 at this step, that means that the guess was incorrect. If the answer was greater than 100, the guess was too low. If your answer was lower than 100, the guess was too high.

Steps to Calculate the Third Level

1. Taking the cashflows of a three-year bond at 6.5%, discount the third-year cashflow with your three guesses shown in Figure 4-4. The cashflows of the bond are shown in Table 4-6. The discounted values, shown in Table 4-7 for Period 3, represent what the bond would be worth two years from now, given the different interest rate scenarios.

Figure 4-4
The Guesses for the Third Node

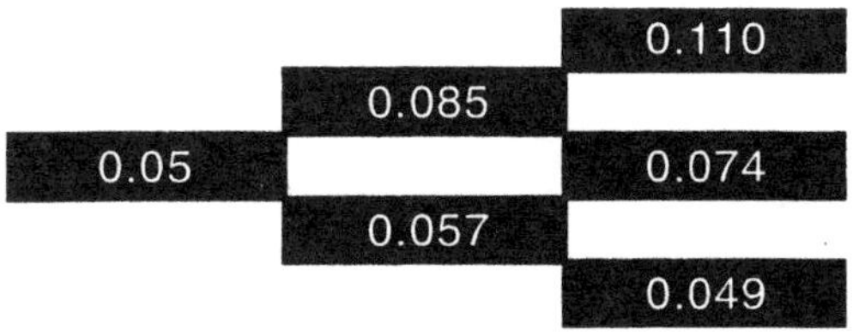

Table 4-6
Cashflows of Three-Year 6.5% Bond

Year	Cashflow
1	\$6.50
2	\$6.50
3	\$106.50

[2]Many of the values in this and subsequent chapters were calculated in a spreadsheet, which carries out numbers to further decimal places than shown in the text. Thus, manual calculations will be slightly off.

Table 4-7

Present Value of Three-Year 6.5% Bond from the Binomial Tree

Period	Lower	Middle	Upper
1		105.000	
2	101.080		95.920
3	101.481	99.182	95.940

2. Add the second period cashflow, $6.50, to the values to obtain $107.981, $105.682, and $102.440. Average the upper and middle values, and the middle and lower values.
3. Discount these two values by the appropriate second node tree yields, to obtain the values shown in period two of Table 4-7.
4. Again, add the first period cashflows to these values. Average the two values, and discount by 5%.

$$\frac{(101.08+6.50)+(95.92+6.50)}{2}=105$$

$$\frac{105}{(1+.05)^1}=100$$

This process can be repeated to create a tree for the entire yield curve.

Jensen's Inequality

Intuitively, we would expect that the average rate for any period in a binomial tree would be equal to that period's forward rate. Compare the average rates for different volatility assumptions in Table 4-8. The third column shows the forward rates. The fourth column shows the average rates for a tree with zero volatility, and the fifth column shows the average rates given 20% volatility. Notice that the fifth column is not equal to the third and fourth columns. Our intuition is incorrect. Why?

Table 4-8

Average Rates for a Binomial Tree

Period	Par Yields	Forward Rates	0% Volatility	20% Volatility
1	6.000	6.000	6.000	6.000
2	9.139	12.371	12.371	12.425
3	11.355	15.924	15.924	16.169
4	13.787	21.406	21.406	22.204

The answer lies in Jensen's Inequality. Jensen's Inequality states that, in general, for an positive random variable $\tilde{X}$,

Equation 4-6
Jensen's Inequality

$$E\left(\frac{1}{\tilde{X}}\right) > \frac{1}{E(\tilde{X})}$$

where E stands for expected value.

When a binomial tree is created using the method outlined in the previous section, the tree's rates are found given today's bond prices. Thus, the tree rates represent an average price, not an average of the rates. This methodology correctly averages different bond prices, as represented on the left side of Equation 4-6. If we, instead, created the binomial tree using the forward rates as the middle path, and then used a volatility assumption to find the branches, we would undervalue the price of the bond as indicated by the inequality. When using bond pricing methodologies other than the binomial tree method, such as Monte Carlo simulation, one must correct for Jensen's Inequality.

Exercise 4-4

Calculate 1/average of X and the average of 1/X where X ={1,5,9}. Repeat this exercise using X ={4,5,6}.

	Set 1	Set 2
avg (x)		
1/av(x)		
avg(1/x)		

Valuing a Bond from a Binomial Tree

A bond can be valued using a binomial tree by following the same process as when creating the tree, the only difference being that no guessing of interest rates is necessary. A binomial tree is very useful to calculate the value of bonds with options.

A Bond with a Call Option

Consider Figure 4-5. The binomial tree is the one calculated in Figure 4-4. The numbers below each yield number correspond to the value of a three-year bond with a 7.5% coupon. The price of the bond today is 102.668. Now, say the bond is callable at the end of year 1 at par. If the bond's value in year 1 is greater than 100, the bond will be called. In Figure 4-6, the outlined node corresponds to where the bond is called. The present value of the bond at the root of the tree has changed from 102.668 to 101.279. This change in value represents the option price, in this case 1.389.

Figure 4-5
Valuation of a Three-Year 7.5% Optionless Bond Using a Binomial Tree

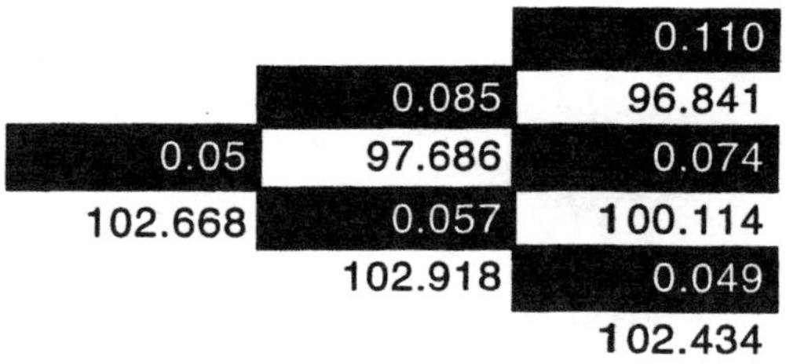

Figure 4-6
Bond Callable at Par at End of First Year

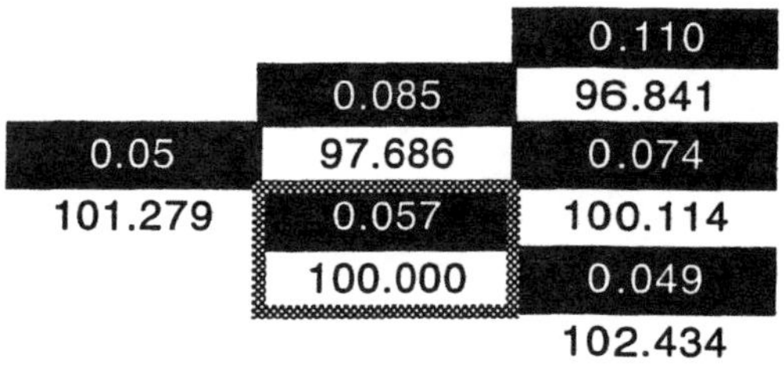

A Bond with a Put Option

Consider Figure 4-7. This tree values the same bond, but with a put option at the end of year 1, instead of a call option. If the price of the bond is less than 100, the option will be exercised. Again, the price change reflects the price of the option, 1.102.

Figure 4-7
Bond Putable at Par at End of First Year

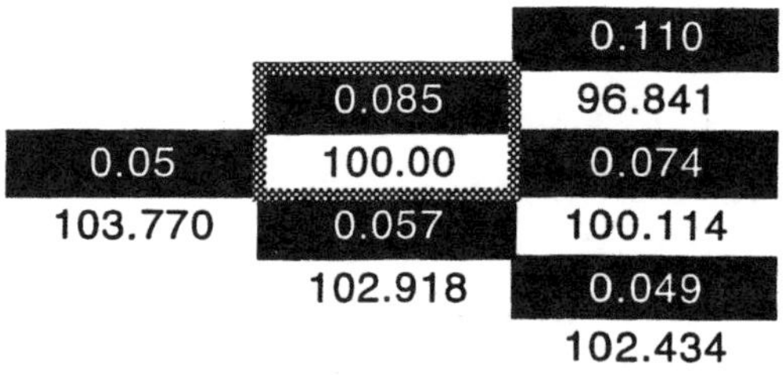

The embedded call options in MBS have a very significant effect on price. An optionless bond will have a positively *convex* price profile.

Figure 4-8 shows the price profile of a 6% bond with and without a call option. The call option can be exercised at par at the end of every period. As interest rates go down, the price of both of the bonds goes up. However, the bond with the call option does not increase in price as rapidly as does the optionless bond. This *concave* curvature for the bond with the call option is termed "negative convexity," which will be described in more detail in Chapter 7.

Figure 4-8

Price Profile of Bond with and without Options

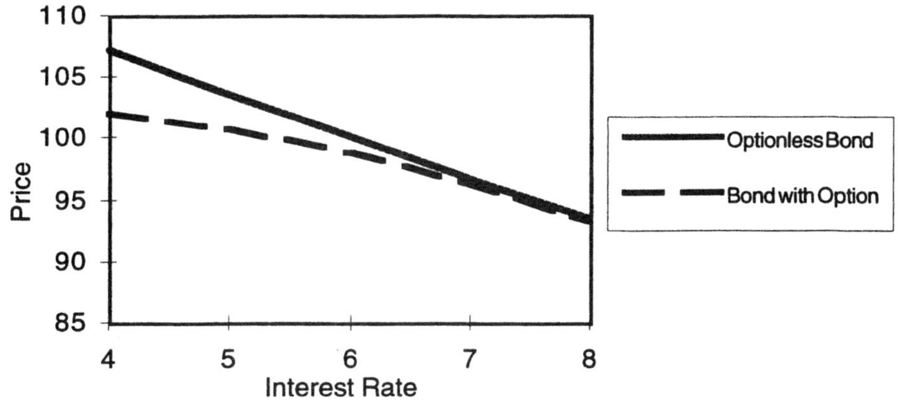

The binomial tree is one method of implementing a single factor term-structure of interest rates. This method offers easy implementation but neglects the role of the yield curve shape on MBS cashflows. Another technical problem is the disregard for path dependency. Multiple factor models using Monte Carlo simulation techniques offer a richer simulation of future yields but at the cost of increased computation time.

Exercise 4-5

Given the following par yield curve, calculate a binomial tree for 15% volatility, and then for 0% volatility.

Period	1	2	3	4
Yield	5.0	5.5	6.5	7.5

Work area

15% Volatility

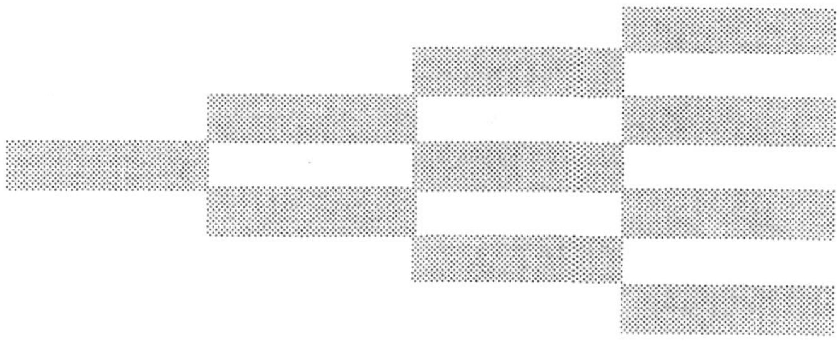

0% Volatility

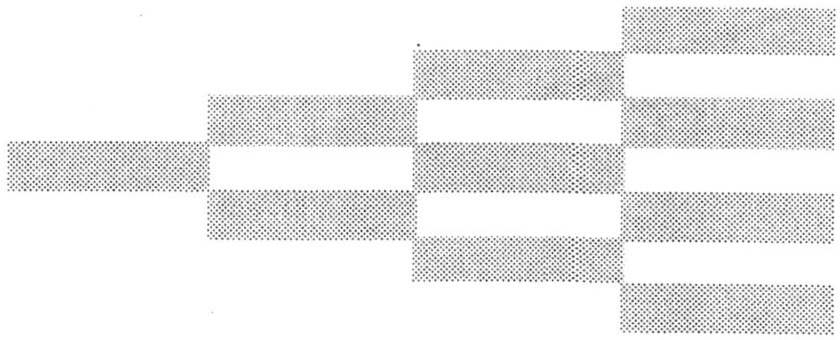

Exercise 4-6

Price a four-year bond with an 8% coupon off of the binomial tree with 15% volatility.

Coupon 8%
15% Volatility

Exercise 4-7

If the bond in Exercise 4-6 has a call option at the end of the third year at par, what is the value of the option? What if it has a put option in the third year at 98?

Bond callable at the end of the third year at par
Option Value:

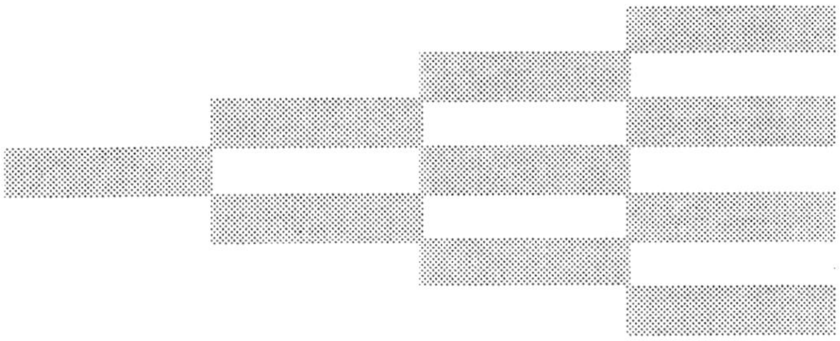

Bond putable at the end of the third year at 98
Option Value:

■ REVIEW QUESTIONS

If the par yield curve is upward sloping, what does that say about spot rates and one period forward rates? Are spot rates higher or lower than par rates? Are forward rates higher or lower than par rates?

If the 30-year zero-coupon bond (strip) has a higher yield than the 30-year coupon bond, is the strip a better investment?

What effect does the volatility assumption have on option value?

Prepayments are linked to a variety of economic factors. How would you incorporate a factor such as GNP growth into a binomial model?

■ ANSWERS TO EXERCISES

4-1

Year of Maturity	**1**	**2**	**3**	**4**
Spot Curve	7.00	8.04	9.13	10.27

	Year Forward		
Maturity	**1**	**2**	**3**
1	9.09	11.33	13.79
2	10.20	12.55	
3	11.38		

4-2

Maturity	**1**	**2**	**3**	**4**
Spot Curve	10.0	9.00	8.00	7.00
Par Curve	10.0	9.04	8.10	7.17

Forward zero rates:

	Year Forward		
Maturity	**1**	**2**	**3**
1	8.01	6.03	4.06
2	7.01	5.04	
3	6.02		

Forward par rates:

	Year Forward		
Maturity	**1**	**2**	**3**
1	8.01	6.03	4.06
2	7.05	5.06	
3	6.10		

4-3

1-Year Volatility:

Date	Yield	Y_i/Y_{i-1}	$\ln(Y_i/Y_{i-1})$
2/13/95	6.82		
2/14/95	6.73	0.987	–0.013
2/15/95	6.64	0.987	–0.013
2/16/95	6.57	0.989	–0.011
2/17/95	6.61	1.006	0.006
2/20/95	6.60	0.998	–0.002
2/21/95	6.65	1.008	0.008
2/22/95	6.46	0.971	–0.029
2/23/95	6.50	1.006	0.006
2/24/95	6.47	0.995	–0.005
Average	**6.605**		**–0.006**
Variance			**0.000**
Daily Stan Dev			**0.012**
Annual			**19.02%**
SD in BP			**125.62**

30-Year Volatility:

Date	Yield	Y_i/Y_{i-1}	$\ln(Y_i/Y_{i-1})$
2/13/95	7.67		
2/14/95	7.61	0.992	–0.008
2/15/95	7.56	0.993	–0.007
2/16/95	7.57	1.001	0.001
2/17/95	7.59	1.003	0.003
2/20/95	7.59	1.000	0.000
2/21/95	7.61	1.003	0.003
2/22/95	7.54	0.991	–0.009
2/23/95	7.55	1.001	0.001
2/24/95	7.53	0.997	–0.003
Average	**7.582**		**–0.002**
Variance			**0.000**
Daily Stan Dev			**0.005**
Annual			**7.44%**
SD in BP			**56.43**

4-4

	Set 1	Set 2
avg (x)	5.000	5.000
1/av(x)	0.200	0.200
avg(1/x)	0.437	0.206

Notice that the inequality is greater as the volatility of x increases.

4-5

15% volatility

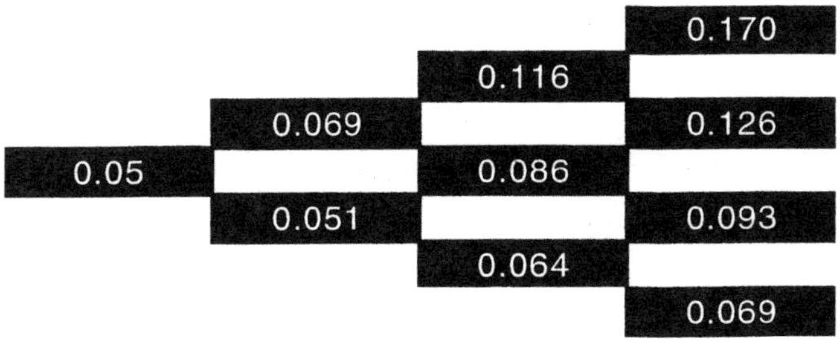

0% Volatility
Note that these are simply the forward rates.

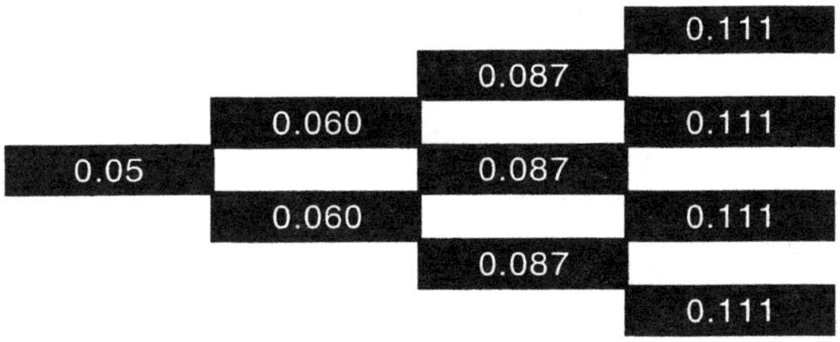

4-6

Coupon 8%
15% Volatility

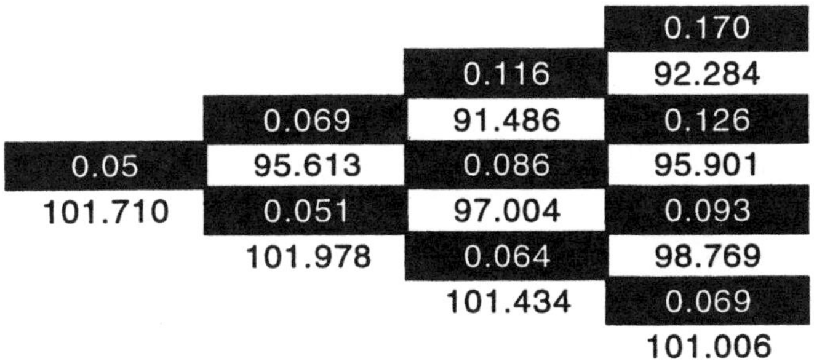

4-7

Bond callable at the end of the third year at par
Option Value: 0.107

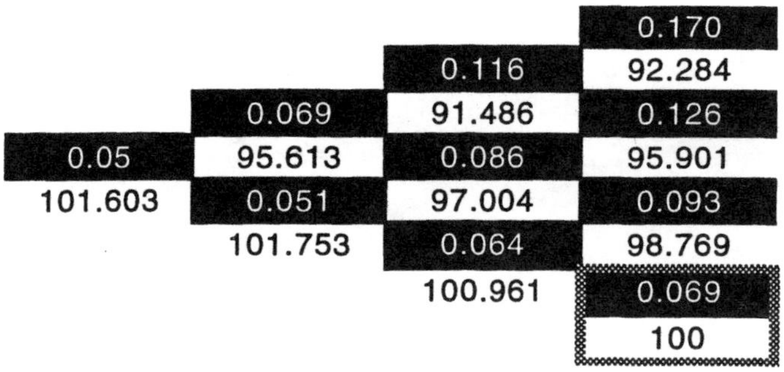

Bond putable at the end of the third year at 98
Option Value: 1.214

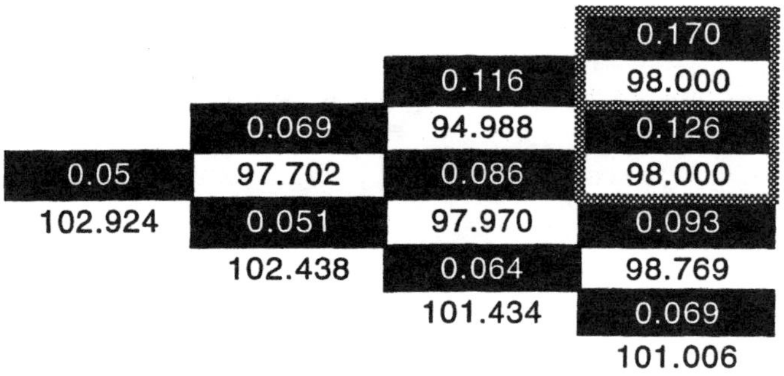

CHAPTER FIVE

Modeling Prepayments

Today some members of the Bulls & Bears MBS research group were coming down to discuss their latest prepayment model. Like the soap companies, the research groups were always promising something "new and improved." The sophisticated statistics indicated that these guys did spend time on the models. But there always seemed to be a gap keeping Susan from putting the models into the simple analytics that she had been building. Maybe the researchers could give a few pointers on some simple modeling techniques. If this went well, she told Bob, the salesman, she'd pick up the tab for lunch.

■ INTRODUCTION

Prepayments are the primary feature of mortgage-backed securities that distinguishes them from all other bonds. Understanding and forecasting prepayments is essential to successful evaluation of mortgage-backed securities as investments. Prepayments represent the actions of individuals and, therefore, forecasting prepayments requires forecasting the aggregate impact of these individual decisions. In this chapter, we look at actual prepayment data. Thorough analysis of the data is required before we even begin the modeling process. We need to understand the limitations of the data while we are identifying the key factors that drive prepayments. This chapter shows how prepayment analysts evaluate data and create prepayment models. In this chapter, we will develop a simple prepayment model that demonstrates several of the principles of prepayment modeling. This model is not intended for actual use in any real investment analysis.

■ SOURCES OF PREPAYMENTS

Prepayments result from four types of events: moving, refinancing, debt retirement, and defaults. Defaults are not actually prepayments; however, most mortgage-backed securities have credit guarantees that transform borrower defaults into prepayments to investors. In order to better understand mortgage-backed securities, it is necessary to understand the conditions under which borrowers will either move, refinance, or default. Because prepayments reflect the actions of individuals, who are driven by a wide variety of economic and social forces, exact predictions are not possible. Prepayment forecasting instead relies on statistical and economic analysis to develop an indication of potential prepayment activity.

■ PURPOSE OF MODELS

Evaluation of the investment characteristics of mortgage-backed securities requires estimates of prepayment rates. These estimates can take various forms, from a single assumption chosen based on experience to complex models that take into account loan level details.

These forecasts, regardless of their source, are used to understand the performance characteristics of mortgage-backed securities and to determine appropriate valuation of different investments.

Prepayment forecasters face a fundamental problem. They seek to estimate future events in a changing world. For example, new loan types are constantly being created and the loan origination process is continually evolving. Still, the primary guide to future prepayments is past prepayments. Thus forecasters develop models that seek to explain prior prepayments. They hope that this information will provide valuable insights into future prepayments. Since the economic and social environment is constantly changing and prepayments are affected by a host of factors, it is unlikely that any historically based analysis will completely reflect future prepayments.

Investing based on prepayment models is a little like driving while looking through the rearview mirror. It may be hard to stay on the road, but it's better than driving with your eyes closed.

Two features that characterize good models are that they are robust and parsimonious. Robust models have the feature that they provide good forecasts under a variety of conditions. That is, they do not need to be continually adjusted to reflect changing environments. If the models need to be changed frequently, then they probably will not provide accurate forecasts of future prepayments. Parsimonious means that the models are as simple as possible. Parsimonious models capture the major variables that affect prepayments using the fewest number of parameters. Parsimonious models have the advantage that they do not "over fit" the data. Using complex models with many parameters, it is possible to set the parameters so that the model provides an excellent fit to historical data, but will not provide accurate projections. The added variables may reflect spurious one-time correlations rather than real long-term relationships. Parsimonious models are also easier to incorporate into valuation tools. In the following pages, we will review the major parameters to be considered and demonstrate how they can be combined to create a prepayment model.

■ PREPAYMENT DATA

The primary consideration when using prepayment data is that you can only evaluate the data that history has provided. In forecasting prepayments, it would be useful to have historical data that demonstrates the prepayment characteristics of loans under a variety of interest rate and economic conditions. Unfortunately, analysis is limited by the actual data that history provides. Figure 5-1 shows the production of new GNMA 30-year loans by year and by coupon. These graphs are contour graphs. They are like looking at mountain ranges from above. From the chart, we can see that there is only a limited range of coupons produced each year. Thus while we might be interested in how GNMA 8s originated in 1989 prepaid in 1992, there is no data available. For other loan types the amount of data might be even more limited. Figure 5-2 shows the loan originations for conventional seven-year balloon loans. Here we can see that there is even less data available to analyze.

Figure 5-1
New GNMA 30-Year Production by Year and Coupon ($ Billion)

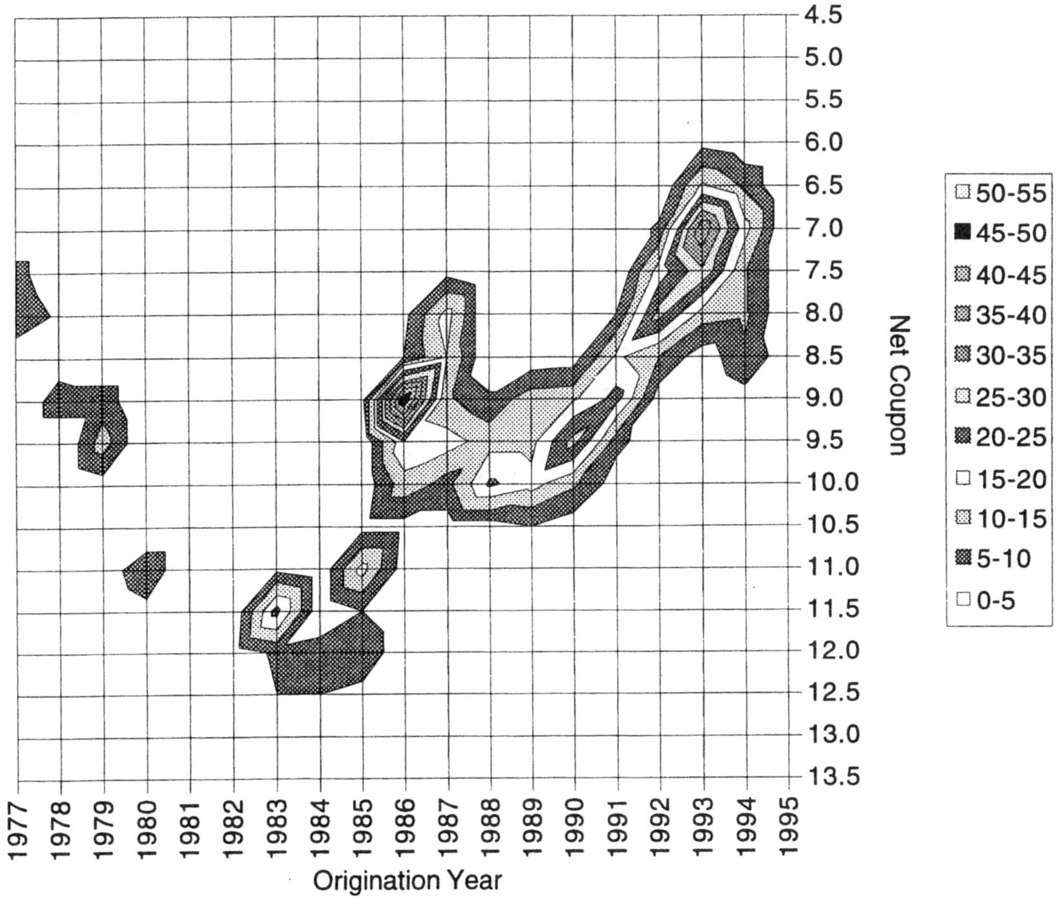

Figure 5-2
Loan Originations for Conventional Seven-Year Balloons ($ Billion)

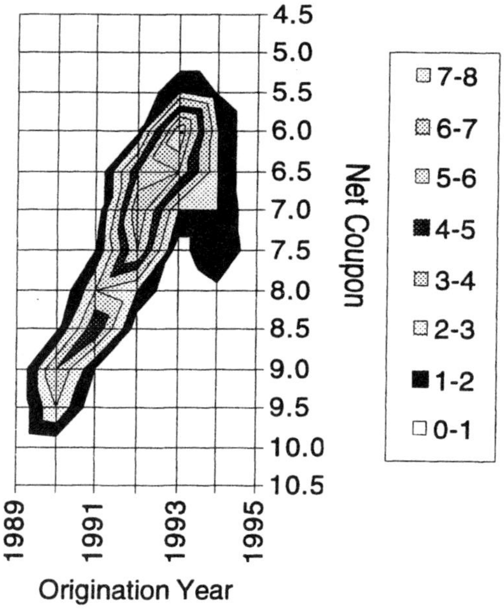

Figure 5-3
Figure 5-1 Data Transformed to Show WAC/CC and Loan Age

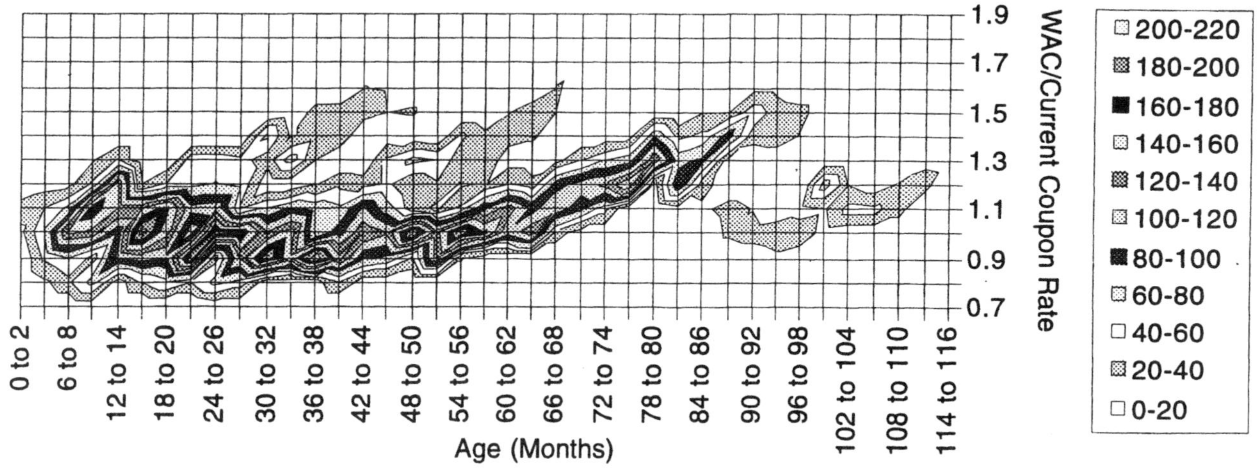

Two of the most important factors in determining prepayment behavior are the interest rate of the loans relative to current market rates and the age of the loan. Figure 5-3 shows the data of Figure 5-1 transformed to show the various combinations of loan coupon relative to the current coupon rate and loan age. The interest rate effect can be represented by comparing the interest rate on the loan to the interest rate on loans currently being originated. The yield on MBS selling just below par, called the current coupon yield, is a good proxy for current mortgage levels. In our analysis we divide the weighted average gross coupons on the loans by the current coupon yield as a measure of the interest rate effect. Loans with higher ratios generally have a greater incentive to prepay. For the GNMA data, we can see that there is a fairly wide range of data available for different combinations of coupon ratio and loan age. However, even for this data set there are limitations.

Exercise 5-1

For what range of loan age is there no data for loans with coupon ratio of 1.1? of 0.9?

Exercise 5-2

What is the highest ratio achieved for loans with ages less than 29 months?

Figure 5-4

Balloon Seven-Year by Age and WAC/CC ($ Billion, PSA categories)

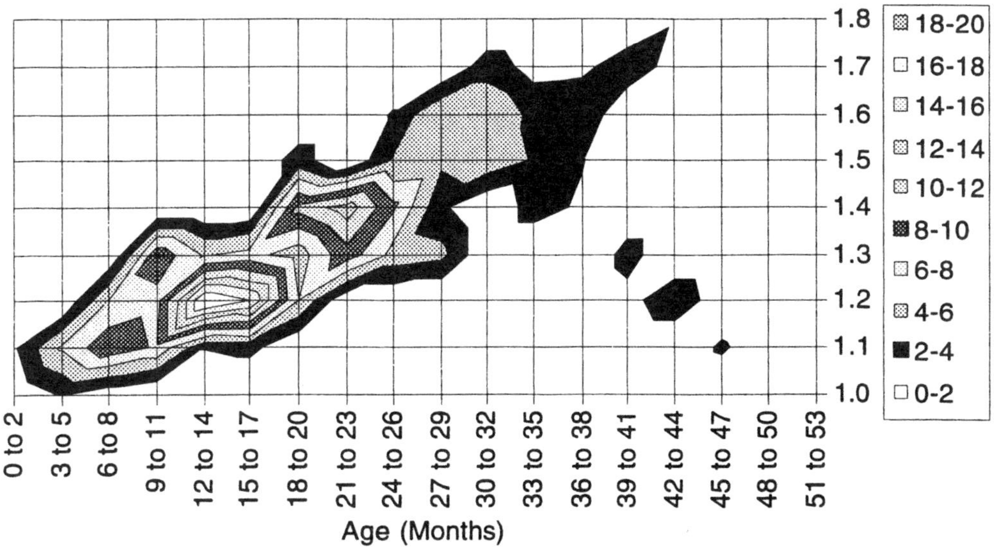

Figure 5-4 shows a similar analysis for the balloon loans in Figure 5-2. Forecasts for data points between existing data points involve interpolation. Forecasts for data points outside the range of existing data points require extrapolation. Generally interpolation is more accurate than extrapolation.

Exercise 5-3

Identify on Figures 5-3 and 5-4 the areas of interpolation and the areas of extrapolation. What does this indicate about the relative reliability of forecasts for GNMA 30-year loans and conventional seven-year balloons? (Keep in mind that the maximum age for the balloon loans is 94 months.)

Viewing prepayment data graphically can often provide insight into prepayment behavior and facilitate prepayment modeling and forecasting. There are two basic types of prepayment graphs that can be examined. The first type is longitudinal or historical data. In this analysis we look at the prepayments on a group of loans or pools over time. This is also sometimes referred to as static pool analysis, because the pool of loans is held constant over time. Figure 5-5 is an example of longitudinal prepayment behavior.

Figure 5-5

Longitudinal Data: Prepayments Over Time for 1989 Originated GNMA 9s

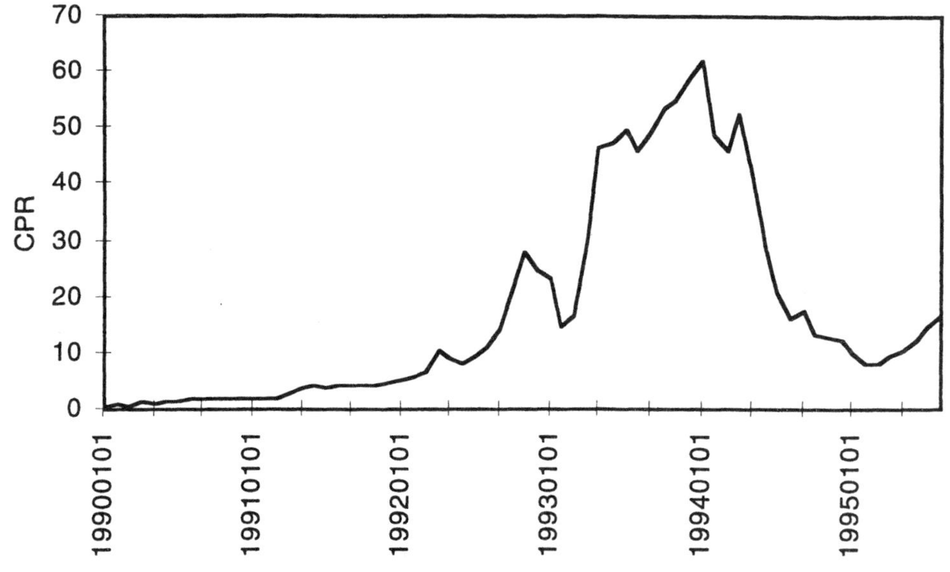

The second type is cross-sectional data. This involves looking at the prepayment rate on different pools of loans, with the data separated by a common characteristic. The most common form of cross sectional data is prepayments by coupon for a given time period. Figure 5-6 shows the one-month prepayment rates on various coupons in the month of April 1993.

Figure 5-6

Cross-Sectional Data: CPR of GNMA 1989 Originations by Coupon

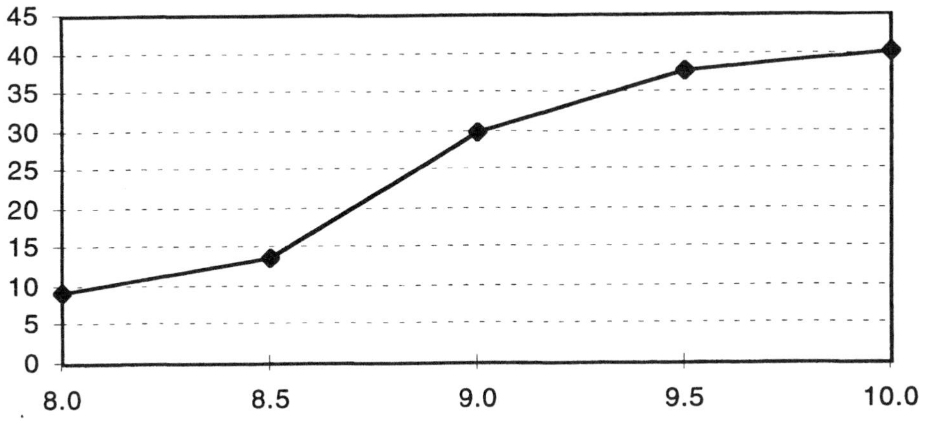

The two graphs produced above are based on the data in Table 5-1. This data is provided so you can learn about prepayment modeling. We do not recommend that any extensive analysis be conducted on this data because it is a relatively small data set. This data should only be used for the exercises in this chapter. The data represents one-month prepayment rates for various GNMA 30-year pools, expressed as CPRs. All of the loans were originated in 1989. The "origination month" indicates the average month of origination. The "current coupon" column represents the monthly average current coupon yield for GNMA 30-year MBS expressed as a bond-equivalent yield.

Table 5-1

GNMA 30-Year Prepayment Data in % CPR

Coupon Orig month	8.0 2/89	8.5 5/89	9.0 8/89	9.5 5/89	10.0 4/89	Current Coupon Yield
19900101	0.7	0.5	0.5	1.6	2.5	9.57
19900201	0.9	0.8	1.1	1.6	2.5	9.83
19900301	0.7	0.7	0.6	2.0	2.7	9.93
19900401	1.4	0.9	1.2	2.5	3.6	10.11
19900501	1.3	0.8	1.0	2.5	3.4	10.10

19900601	1.8	1.4	1.4	2.9	4.2	9.78
19900701	1.4	1.4	1.6	3.4	4.4	9.67
19900801	1.2	1.8	1.8	3.1	4.7	9.83
19900901	2.2	1.7	1.9	3.6	5.4	9.91
19901001	1.7	1.6	1.7	3.3	4.3	9.90
19901101	3.0	4.2	2.0	3.3	4.9	9.59
19901201	1.8	1.7	1.7	2.9	4.5	9.24
19910101	1.8	1.9	2.0	3.7	4.9	9.17
19910201	1.9	1.7	1.8	2.6	4.5	8.86
19910301	1.5	2.2	1.9	3.2	5.2	9.13
19910401	2.5	2.9	2.8	4.4	6.7	9.06
19910501	3.5	7.0	3.6	5.4	8.9	9.07
19910601	3.9	4.1	4.3	6.1	9.7	9.26
19910701	3.6	3.2	4.0	6.5	9.7	9.15
19910801	3.2	3.3	4.1	6.4	8.6	8.73
19910901	3.0	4.2	4.2	6.4	8.6	8.48
19911001	4.4	3.2	4.1	5.7	7.9	8.31
19911101	4.1	3.4	4.4	6.9	11.9	8.22
19911201	3.9	4.2	4.6	8.0	16.2	7.82
19920101	3.9	4.2	5.3	10.2	20.9	7.80
19920201	4.4	5.3	5.9	12.6	23.5	8.15
19920301	4.3	4.7	6.5	18.9	30.0	8.38
19920401	6.1	6.2	10.2	24.0	39.6	8.26
19920501	7.3	5.6	9.0	20.3	33.6	8.14
19920601	7.3	7.1	8.2	16.4	27.3	7.96
19920701	7.7	6.5	9.4	18.0	26.3	7.48
19920801	7.4	7.6	10.7	19.2	26.5	7.29
19920901	7.1	7.0	14.2	25.9	29.2	7.30
19921001	6.3	9.1	21.6	37.5	37.9	7.61
19921101	8.0	11.0	28.0	43.6	43.6	7.88
19921201	8.7	10.4	24.5	38.7	40.2	7.68
19930101	7.9	10.4	23.1	38.5	44.5	7.42
19930201	6.3	6.0	14.9	25.3	31.0	7.11
19930301	5.8	6.0	16.8	25.6	29.6	6.89
19930401	9.4	13.7	29.9	37.7	40.0	6.90
19930501	10.8	27.5	46.4	49.4	48.9	6.96
19930601	15.1	28.6	47.3	49.9	47.3	6.81

19930701	16.4	33.2	49.5	52.8	51.4	6.61
19930801	16.1	31.4	45.7	50.0	46.8	6.52
19930901	17.6	35.6	49.2	48.3	47.5	6.21
19931001	24.2	39.4	53.4	51.9	49.3	6.22
19931101	28.6	46.5	54.9	52.5	48.8	6.69
19931201	34.5	50.6	58.9	54.3	53.3	6.68
19940101	33.8	49.9	62.0	60.5	57.6	6.53
19940201	23.7	36.5	48.6	48.9	49.3	6.80
19940301	23.6	34.1	45.8	46.3	45.2	7.46
19940401	25.4	39.0	52.6	53.8	54.6	8.07
19940501	18.3	24.8	41.6	46.7	50.7	8.25
19940601	17.5	19.0	28.5	34.7	41.8	8.13
19940701	12.5	15.7	20.9	27.1	33.5	8.34
19940801	10.8	11.9	16.1	23.0	27.3	8.27
19940901	11.0	14.0	17.3	20.9	25.0	8.47
19941001	11.7	8.6	13.2	19.5	22.2	8.80
19941101	8.1	8.8	12.9	16.7	21.3	9.00
19941201	8.8	9.4	12.5	14.7	17.7	8.91
19950101	9.5	7.3	9.9	12.8	17.6	8.82
19950201	5.9	5.1	8.0	9.7	13.8	8.49
19950301	5.8	6.4	7.8	9.1	11.7	8.22
19950401	8.2	10.6	9.5	12.2	13.2	8.11
19950501	7.8	8.4	10.6	12.6	16.1	7.69
19950601	12.0	11.4	12.2	14.8	16.0	7.34
19950701	12.2	12.4	14.9	16.3	18.7	7.41
19950801	11.4	14.6	16.6	16.9	18.5	7.63

Source: Bloomberg Financial Markets.

Interest Rate Effect

The primary factor that influences prepayment rates is the borrower's opportunity to refinance. This is reflected by the coupon on the borrower's loan versus the interest rate currently available in the market for new loans. We use the yield on mortgage-backed securities trading near par, sometimes called the current coupon yield, as a proxy for the rates available to borrowers. The relationship between the mortgage coupon and the current coupon yield can be reflected either as a difference or as a ratio. Loans where the difference between the loan coupon and the current coupon is greater than zero or where the ratio is above one have a greater incentive to refinance.

Figure 5-7 is a cross-sectional analysis of prepayment rates as a function of the coupon on the loan relative to the current coupon yield. Note that prepayment rates are relatively stable when the coupon on the mortgage is below the current coupon yield, but then increase rapidly as the incentive to refinance to a lower coupon loan increases. The prepayment rate then peaks and begins to fall off.

Figure 5-7
Cross-Sectional Data Showing the Interest Rate Effect

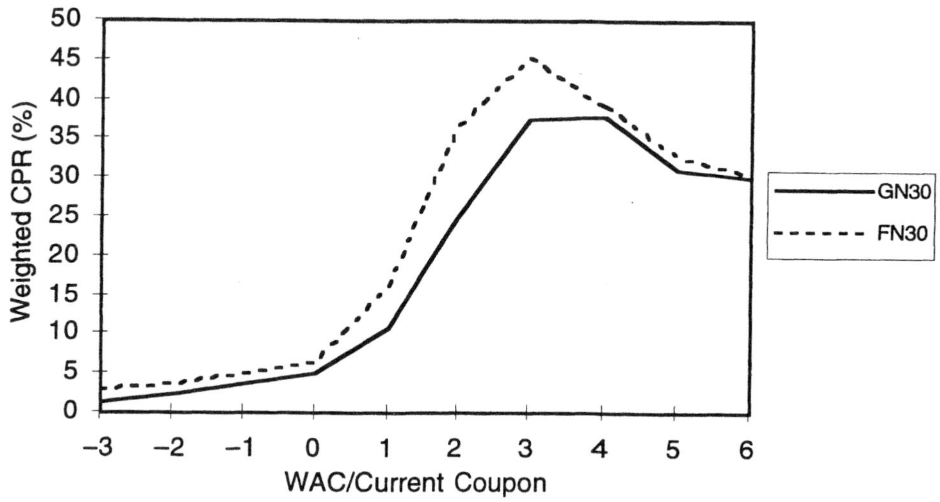

■ REVIEW QUESTION

Issues to think about: Do borrowers with very high coupon differences relative to the current coupon yield (greater than 300 basis points) have less incentive to refinance than borrowers with lower coupon differences? What accounts for the dip in the prepayment curve?

One approach to modeling prepayments is to choose a functional form that reflects the analysts' view of the relationship between the variables. The analyst then attempts to find parameter values that match the function to the data. This is normally done using sophisticated statistical packages. This process is complicated by nonlinear interactions between the factors driving prepayments. Below we will present a very simplified functional form that represents the product of functions for each of the individual factors.

The arctangent function is a convenient nonlinear representation for the shape of the prepayment curve. At one point, many analysts used this function. Now, however, it has been replaced by more complex functional forms. The arctangent function has the shape shown in Figure 5-8. Note the similarity between this shape and Figure 5-7. While the arctangent function has the same general shape as the prepayment curve, it goes through different points.

Figure 5-8
The Arctangent Function

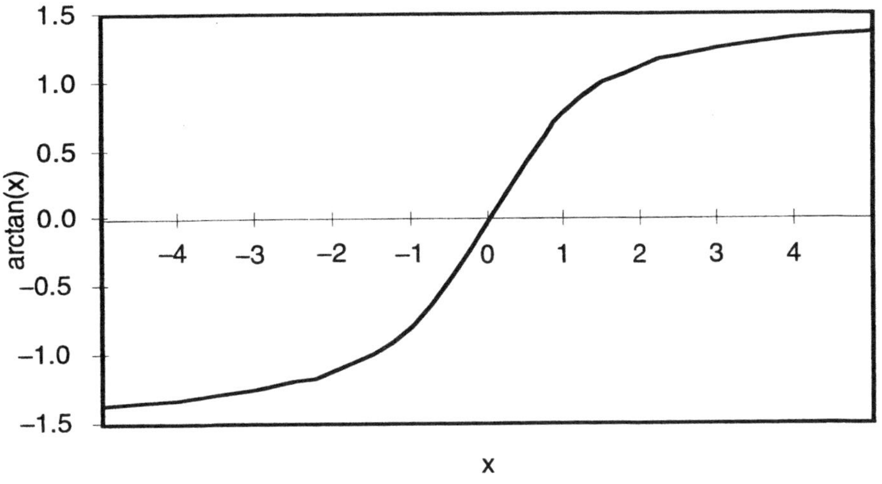

In order to use the arctangent function for prepayment analysis, it is necessary to transform the function to match the prepayment curve. The arctangent function can be transformed by using a function of the form:

$$\text{Interest Rate Effect} = a + b \times (\arctan(c + d \times (\text{diff})))$$

Equation 5-1
Arctangent Function Transformation for Interest Rate Effect

where a, b, c, and d are constants and diff is the difference between the coupon on the loan and the current coupon yield expressed in basis points. The constants a, b, c, and d need to be chosen in order to match the arctangent curve to the prepayment data. Equation 5-1 has four constants (a, b, c, and d); therefore we need four points on the prepayment curve to solve for these values.

Exercise 5-4

Solve for a, b, c, and d in Equation 5-1. (Note: In Excel, the arctangent function is atan(x)).

Assume:

1. The maximum CPR is 50%.
2. The minimum CPR is 6%.
3. The midpoint 28% CPR occurs at diff = 200 basis points.
4. At midpoint, max slope is 6% CPR for a 10 basis point rate shift.

Using a little algebra and calculus, Equation 5-1 gives the following relationships:

1. $a = (\text{max CPR} + \text{min CPR})/2$.
2. $b = (\text{max CPR} - a)/(\pi/2)$.
3. $d = \text{max slope}/b$.
4. $c = -d \times \text{midpoint diff}$.

Note: More advanced readers can derive these equations.

Based on these equations solve for a, b, c, and d. Note that this is not an actual prepayment function. While these numbers are similar to GNMA prepayment estimates the results are only intended as an example of how to fit the arctangent curve to prepayment data. Solve these equations using prepayment rates in percent (i.e. 50%) and rate changes in basis points (i.e. 200 bp).

Work area

a =
b =
c =
d =

Exercise 5-5

Using the data in Table 5-1, reproduce Figure 5-7. The first step is to compute the relative coupon for each prepayment observation. Next it is necessary to place the prepayment rates in buckets for each range. For example, coupon differentials of 0.76 to 1.25 can go in the 100 basis point difference bucket. Finally an average for each bucket can be calculated.

There is usually a time lag between changes in interest rates and changes in prepayment rates. Figure 5-9 demonstrates this effect. Note how interest rates changed in September 1993 followed by a change in prepayment rates three months later. Using Figure 5-9, see if you can find another period when rates moved rapidly and the change in prepayment rates occurred later.

Figure 5-9

A Time Lag Between Interest Rate Changes and Prepayment Rates

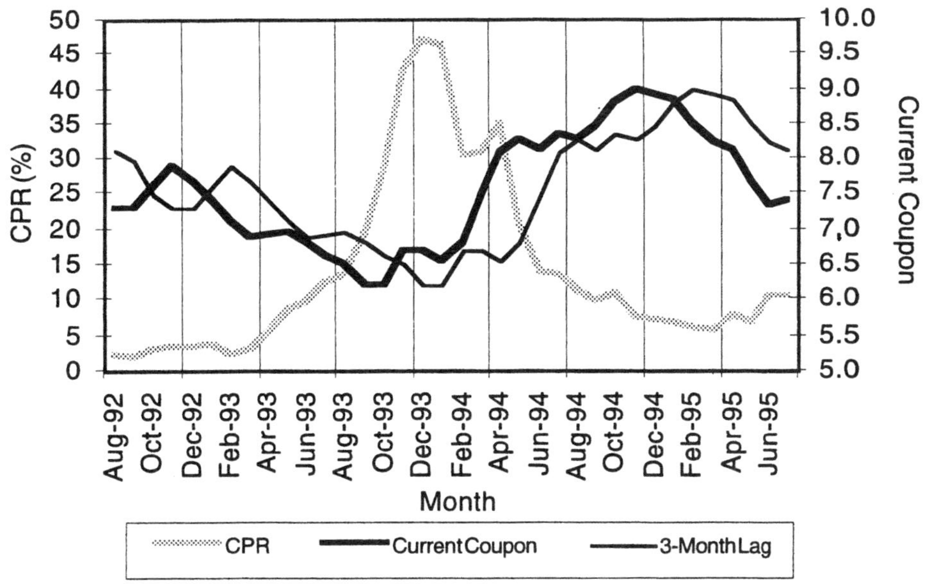

REVIEW QUESTION

How would you change the method in Exercise 5-5 to reflect this lag effect? Many investors rely on current prepayment data as an indication of future prepayments. When is this most likely to be unreliable?

Aging

The second major component of prepayment behavior is aging. Aging reflects the observation that newer loans tend to prepay slower than older or "seasoned" loans. Figure 5-10 shows the prepayment rate of FNMA 30-year loans by loan age. The chart splits out loans by discount coupon, low premium coupons, and high premium coupons. The discount loans reach their peak prepayment speeds after 30 months. The low premiums reach their peak speed at about 27 months, while the high premiums peak in about 21 months. The PSA curve is used to approximate this effect. The graph, however, makes it clear that not all loans reach their peak speed in 30 months as assumed by the PSA curve.

Figure 5-10

Aging Effect for Current Coupon and Medium and High Premium Loans

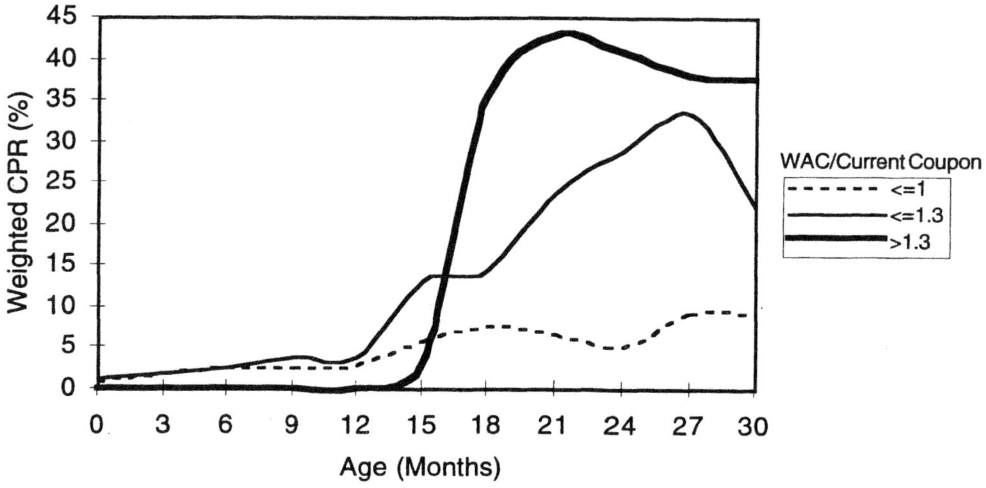

Exercise 5-6

Graph the prepayment data in Table 5-1 by loan age. (A graph by "as of date" will approximate a graph by loan age, since all the loans were originated within a few months of each other.)

Aging can be reflected in the formula:

Equation 5-2
An Aging Formula

$$\text{Age \%} = \min\left[\frac{\text{age}}{\text{e}}, 1\right]$$

where age is the age of the loan in months and e is a constant. A standard assumption, consistent with the PSA model is that e = 30.

Burnout

The third factor affecting prepayments is burnout. This is perhaps the most complex of the components. Burnout reflects the observation that as interest rates drop, prepayments for a pool of loans peak and then decline. Even if rates fall further, later prepayments do not reach the earlier peaks. Figure 5-11 demonstrates this effect. This graph shows prepayments on FNMA 11.5s originated in 1985. Prepayment rates peaked near 60% CPR in the summer of 1987. They then declined rapidly, reflecting burnout and higher interest rate levels. In 1992 the burnout effect is clear. Even though rates fell below the levels of 1987, prepayments did not reach the same peak level and were unable to sustain rates over 40% CPR despite substantially lower interest rate levels.

Figure 5-11
Burnout Effect Using Longitudinal Data

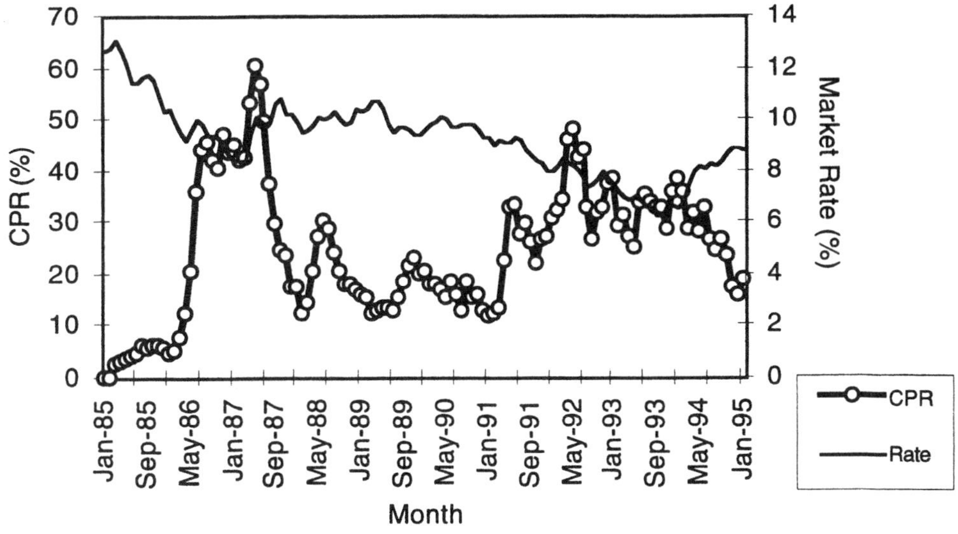

A simple example of burnout is shown in Figure 5-12. Suppose a pool of 100 loans is made of 80 fast prepayers who prepay at 75% per year and 20 slow prepayers who prepay at 10% per year. During the first period, you would expect prepayments of 62% (0.80 × 75% + .20 × 10%). After one year, three quarters of the fast prepayers are gone. Only 10% of the slow prepayers have prepaid. The remaining composition is 20 fast and 18 slow. The new expected prepayment rate is about 44%.

For our model we can use a simple functional form that describes burnout as a function of the pool factor.

Equation 5-3
A Burnout Formula

$$\text{Burn } \% = 1 - f \times (1 - \text{factor})$$

where f is a constant parameter of the model and "factor" is the pool factor. We will assume for our model that f = 0.7.

Figure 5-12
A Burnout Example

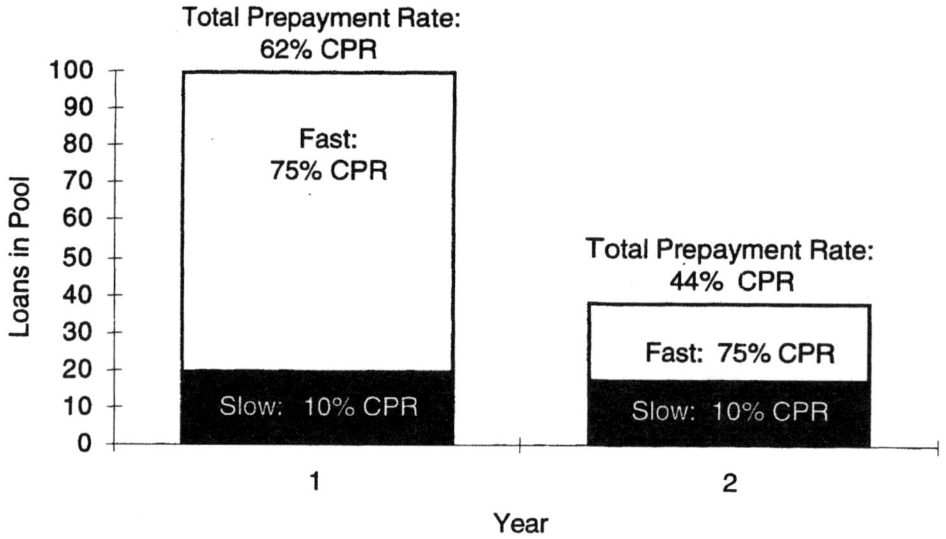

Exercise 5-7

What happens to the usefulness of this equation in forecasting burnout, if the pool consists of loans that were seasoned before they were pooled? Hint: the pool factor is 1 when the pool is created, regardless of the age of the loans.

Seasonality

The fourth factor affecting prepayment rates is seasonality. One of the sources of prepayments is housing turnover. This economic activity is seasonal due to weather, school schedules, and possibly, tax considerations. The seasonality of housing turnover is clearly seen in the prepayment data. Figure 5-13 shows the prepayment rates for discount conventional loans during 1987-1990. Prepayment seasonality is reflected in the pattern showing higher prepayment rates in the late summer and lower prepayment rates in the winter.

Figure 5-13
Prepayment Seasonality

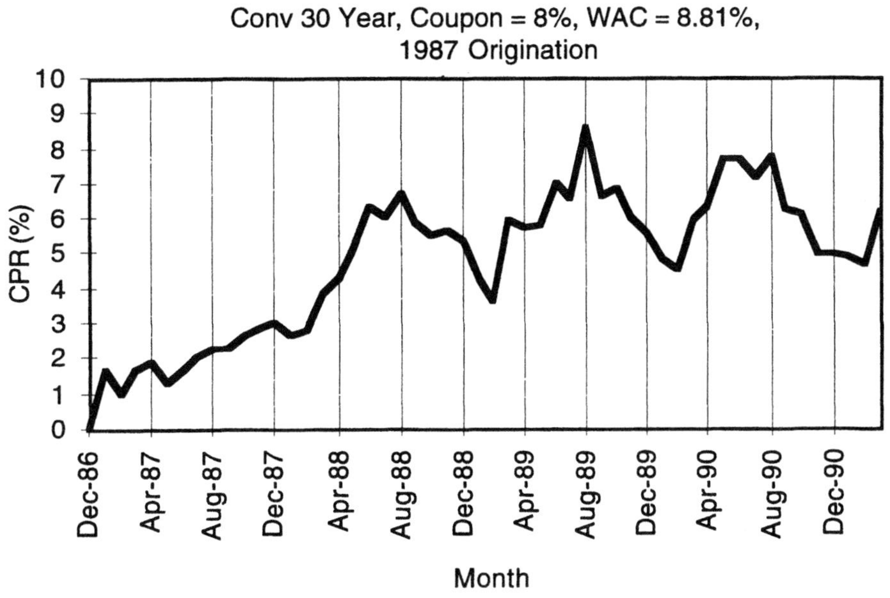

Exercise 5-8

Using the data below, calculate the average prepayment rate for each month of the year. Divide these average rates for each month by the overall average prepayment for all the data to produce monthly adjustments.

Work area

Month	89 8.0s	90 8.0s	89 8.5s	90 8.5s	Average	Factor
Jan	4.19	4.79	4.93	5.58	4.87	0.75
Feb	3.61	4.54	4.96	5.40		
Mar	5.91	5.95	6.08	6.72		
Apr	5.73	6.33	6.49	7.47		
May	5.79	7.69	6.86	8.05		
June	6.97	7.69	7.28	8.32		
July	6.56	7.15	7.46	7.96		
Aug	8.56	7.71	8.68	8.80		
Sep	6.62	6.21	7.77	7.20		
Oct	6.81	6.12	7.46	7.39		
Nov	5.98	5.00	6.67	5.71		
Dec	5.54	4.93	6.67	5.74		
Average	6.02	6.18	6.78	7.03		

In prepayment models, seasonality is often reflected as a lookup function, where the seasonal effect is found on a table:

Equation 5-4
Seasonality as a Lookup Function

$$\text{Seasonal (month)} = \text{Result from table for month}$$

Other Factors

Prepayments are also affected by a variety of other factors. Some of these include loan size, loan-to-value ratios, local employment levels, points paid at origination, and availability of other loan types. Virtually any factor that affects homeowners could have an impact on prepayments. Prepayment models can be developed to include these factors.

Building a Simple Prepayment Model

The factors and formulas that we have discussed above can be combined together to produce an overall model to describe and forecast prepayment behavior. In a sophisticated model these factors may interact with complex relationships between them. In addition, other factors may also be used in the model. Figure 5-11, shown earlier, in addition to demonstrating burnout, combines elements of all of the factors we have considered so far. See if you can identify them in the graph.

For our purposes here we will construct a simple prepayment model using Formulas 5-1 through 5-4 above. This model is *not* intended for actual analysis. The form of the model is that the effects are all multiplicative:

Equation 5-5
Simple Prepayment Model

$$\text{Interest(diff)} \times \text{Age\%(age)} \times \text{Burn\%(factor)} \times \text{Seasonal(month)}$$

Exercise 5-9

Use the parameter values established above and fill out the following table using the inputs given below. Be sure to convert the coupon difference to basis points before using Equation 5-1.

Current Coupon	WAC	Age	Factor	Month
8	9	24	0.9	Jan
7	9	50	0.8	Jul
6	9	75	0.7	Mar
8	10	50	0.6	Feb
9	7	10	0.8	Oct
7	14	120	0.4	Nov

Work area

Interest	Age	Burnout	Seasonal	Total

Table 5-2 is an example of actual forecasts for December as of December 15, 1995. These forecasts represent the median forecast of several dealers who post their prepayment forecasts on Bloomberg. Note how the forecasts follow somewhat the same pattern seen in Figure 5-7.

Table 5-2
Sample Forecasts from the Bloomberg

Coupon	GNMA 30-Year	FNMA/ FHLMC 30-Year
6.0	98	134
6.5	110	140
7.0	129	171
7.5	167	213
8.0	212	280
8.5	277	332
9.0	315	347
9.5	314	347
10.0	323	354
10.5	309	359
11.0	280	331

Source: Bloomberg Financial Markets.

Prepayment forecasting is a combination of economics, psychology, and statistics. The work of prepayment analysis is never complete. Innovations in mortgage products and the changing dynamics of borrowers and originators mean that every new piece of data adds to our understanding of prepayments. This exciting dynamic adds to the complexity and challenge of investing in mortgage-backed securities.

Figure 5-14
Dealer Median Prepayment Date from Table 5-2

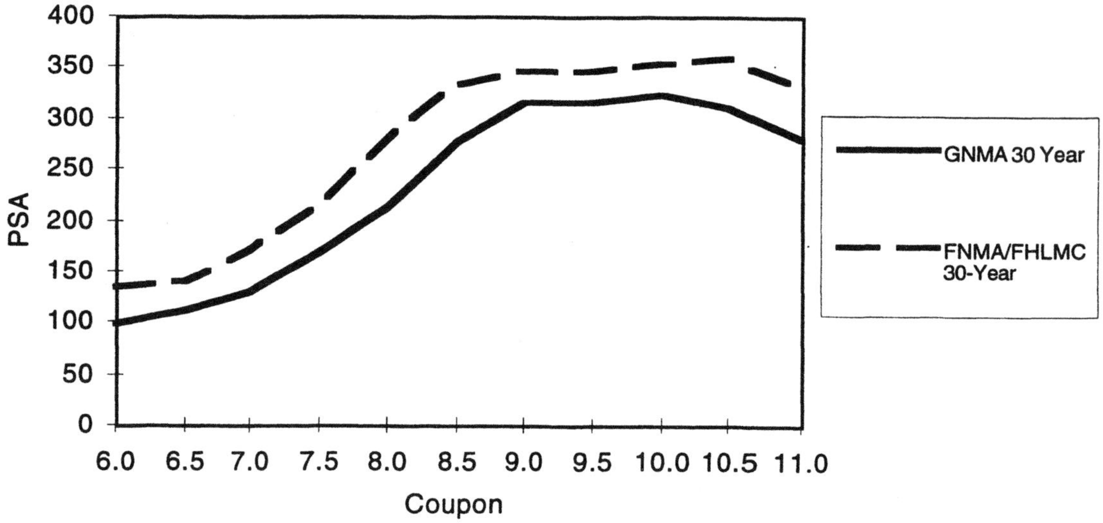

Source: Bloomberg Financial Markets.

■ ANSWERS TO EXERCISES

5-1

Ratio of 1.1: 75-86, 111+

Ratio of 0.9: 0-2, 57+

5-2

The highest ratio is approximately 1.36.

5-3

Forecasts for current coupon new loans or premium older 7-year balloons should be fairly reliable. Outside this range, say for 27-month current coupon loans, forecasts would not be very reliable since there is no data. GNMA 30-year loans have a much larger data set including some high discount to high premium loans for a variety of ages. Thus, one would expect GNMA forecasts to be more reliable.

5-4

a	28.0%
b	14.0%
c	–8.571
d	0.043

5-5

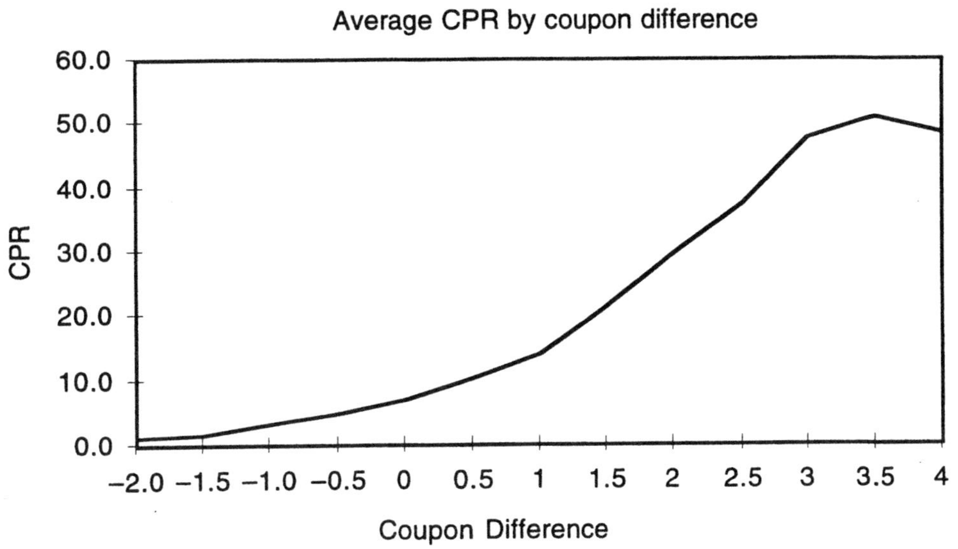
Average CPR by coupon difference
60.0
50.0
40.0
30.0
20.0
10.0
0.0
CPR
−2.0 −1.5 −1.0 −0.5 0 0.5 1 1.5 2 2.5 3 3.5 4
Coupon Difference

5-6

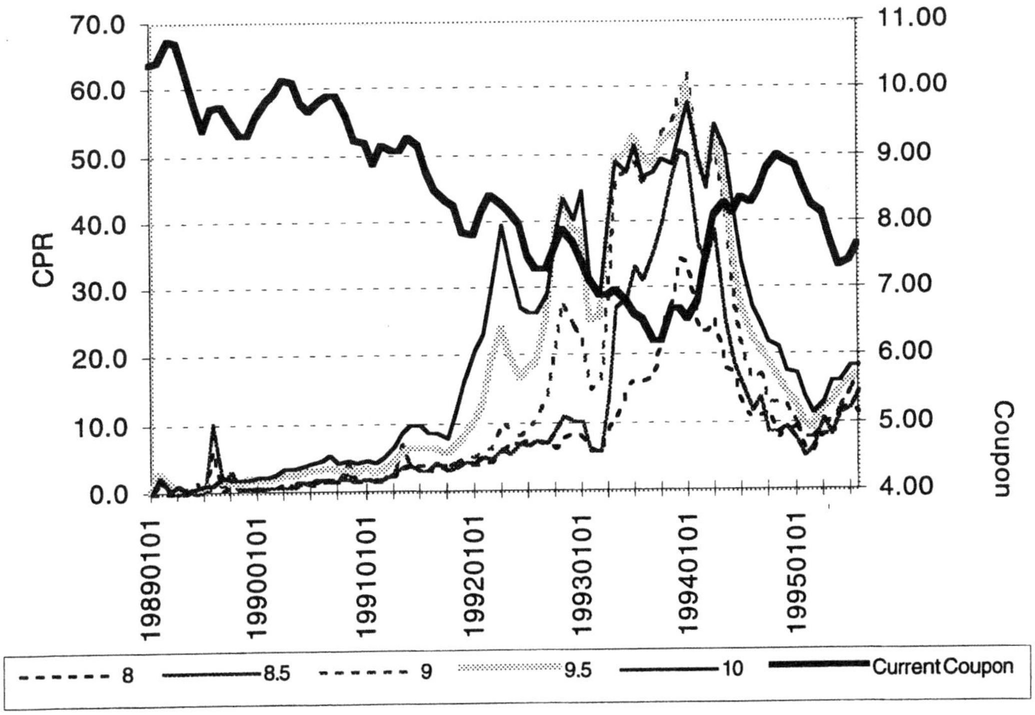
70.0
60.0
50.0
40.0
30.0
20.0
10.0
0.0
CPR
11.00
10.00
9.00
8.00
7.00
6.00
5.00
4.00
Coupon
19890101
19900101
19910101
19920101
19930101
19940101
19950101
8
8.5
9
9.5
10
Current Coupon

5-7

Generally, the pool will be more "burned-out" than the Burn% calculation indicates. The prepayment forecasts from the model will be higher than if the loans were pooled when new. There are many other variables that affect burnout other than the pool factor that should be considered in a sophisticated prepayment model.

5-8

Month	89 8.0s	90 8.0s	89 8.5s	90 8.5s	Average	Factor
Jan	4.19	4.79	4.93	5.58	4.87	0.75
Feb	3.61	4.54	4.96	5.40	4.63	0.71
Mar	5.91	5.95	6.08	6.72	6.17	0.95
Apr	5.73	6.33	6.49	7.47	6.51	1.00
May	5.79	7.69	6.86	8.05	7.10	1.09
June	6.97	7.69	7.28	8.32	7.57	1.16
July	6.56	7.15	7.46	7.96	7.28	1.12
Aug	8.56	7.71	8.68	8.80	8.44	1.30
Sep	6.62	6.21	7.77	7.20	6.95	1.07
Oct	6.81	6.12	7.46	7.39	6.95	1.07
Nov	5.98	5.00	6.67	5.71	5.84	0.90
Dec	5.54	4.93	6.67	5.74	5.72	0.88
Average	6.02	6.18	6.78	7.03	6.50	1.00

5-9

Interest	Age	Burnout	Seasonal	Total
9.2%	0.80	0.93	0.75	5.13%
28.0%	1.00	0.86	1.12	26.97%
46.8%	1.00	0.79	0.95	35.12%
28.0%	1.00	0.72	0.71	14.31%
6.8%	0.33	0.86	1.07	2.09%
49.3%	1.00	0.58	0.90	25.73%

CHAPTER SIX

CMOs, IOs, and POs, and Structuring

Like sharks on the blood trail, the Street had found out that Susan had a good bid for MBS. She was being shown lots of secondary bonds as well as new CMOs. With the secondary bonds, there seemed to be some tools available to look at risk and return. However, with the new issues, all she had were the price/yield tables. She really felt uncomfortable using these for investment decisions. It was a bit like buying shoes through a catalog. Small changes in the cut and style could make an expensive purchase uncomfortable. To make a decision she needed to try the bond on for size—manipulate the cashflows. Buying a structuring model was too expensive. Maybe she could just develop some simple tools to carve up the cashflows.

■ INTRODUCTION

Collateralized Mortgage Obligations (CMOs) facilitate the distribution of the vast amount of mortgage debt. The CMO structuring process creates bonds with a variety of investment characteristics that are different from the underlying collateral. These bonds can be distributed to investors who have a variety of investment needs. Bonds can be created with differing average lives, coupons, and prepayment sensitivities. This variety of investment products serves to expand the demand for mortgage-backed securities.

The motivation for creating CMOs is arbitrage. Wall Street dealers seek to create CMOs when the value of the CMO bonds exceeds the value of the mortgage collateral used to create the CMO plus any expenses. CMO bonds, created by Wall Street, must compete with other fixed-income securities in investor portfolios. Each CMO bond has specific investment characteristics that may be similar to other fixed-income securities. By transforming mortgages into bonds with characteristics more like other securities, the CMO market serves to link the MBS market to other fixed-income markets.

One motivating factor for the development of the CMO market was the ability to distribute comparatively uniform mortgage-backed securities to a diverse investor base. Investors were willing to pay more for bonds that met their investment needs. Another source of arbitrage was the difficulty of analyzing some high risk/high yield CMOs, creating uncertainty about fair value.

CMO creation is subject to a variety of legal and tax issues. The most important considerations are the Real Estate Mortgage Investment Conduit (REMIC) regulations. These are a set of tax rules that allow CMOs to avoid taxation at the trust level, which would otherwise make CMOs uneconomical to create. The rules distinguish between two types of securities, regular interests and residual interests. Each must meet certain requirements. The bonds that we discuss below would usually be structured as regular interests.

■ CMOS AS RULES

CMO bonds are created by distributing the cashflow of the underlying mortgage-backed securities according to a set of rules. These rules describe how principal is allocated among the various CMO bonds and how interest is allocated among the bonds. Principal and interest can be allocated using a variety of rules. While an infinite variety of rules is theoretically possible, most CMOs are created using a few standard types. For principal payments these include: sequential, pro-rata, and scheduled. For interest payments they include: fixed, floating, inverse-floating, and accrual. Most CMOs are created through combinations and layering of these structuring methods.

Constructing a CMO

In this chapter, we construct simple CMOs using principal and interest pay types described above. These exercises build on previous chapters.

The chapter contains two parallel sets of exercises. A simplified method demonstrates the main principles, but omits some of the details. The second method, a more detailed approach uses the standard mortgage cashflow calculations discussed in earlier chapters. The more detailed approach is best performed on a spreadsheet or using a programming language. Readers may perform either set of exercises or both. There are also advanced questions and exercises for which we have not provided answers. These questions are intended to provoke thought about some of the more complex issues in CMOs.

The simplified CMO model uses the following assumptions:

Annual cashflows.

Annual interest payments.

Annual prepayment as a percentage of original balance (APP).

Five-year maturity, no amortization.

No servicing fee for loans.

The spreadsheet model uses the following more realistic assumptions:

Monthly cashflows.

Monthly interest payments.

PSA model for prepayments.

30-year level pay mortgages.

Net coupon and gross coupon.

Step 1 Create the Cashflows of the Underlying Securities

The structure of any CMO is dependent on the cashflows of the underlying mortgage pool. The cashflows from Exercise 6-1 will form the basis for all the CMOs that we create in this chapter.

Exercise 6-1

Simple CMO Model:

Assume an initial balance of $100 million dollars (in millions).

Assume a security coupon of 10%.

Assume that the loan matures in five years and has no principal amortization.

Assume prepayments are stated as an annual percentage of the original balance (APP).[1] For example a 15% APP means that $15 million prepays each year.

Spreadsheet Model:

Use the cashflow model created in Chapter 3.

Assume an initial balance of $100 million.

Assume a net coupon of 10% and a gross coupon of 10.65%.

Assume a maturity of 30 years.

Exercise 6-1a (Simple CMO Model)

Calculate the cashflows of the mortgages assuming a 10% APP, 20% APP, and 30% APP. Show the principal and interest cashflows separately.

[1]APP is similar to the "ABS" method used for asset-backed securities.

Exercise 6-1b (Simple CMO Model)

Compute the average life of the mortgages for 10% APP, 20% APP and 30% APP.

Work area

Underlying Security	
Balance	100
Coupon	10
Maturity	5

APP 10%

Year	Balance	Principal	Interest	Cashflow
1	100	10	10	20
2				
3				
4				
5				
6				
Avg Life				

APP 20%

Year	Balance	Principal	Interest	Cashflow
1	100			
2				
3				
4				
5				
6				
Avg Life				

APP 30%

Year	Balance	Principal	Interest	Cashflow
1	100			
2				
3				
4				
5				
6				
Avg Life				

Exercise 6-1c (Spreadsheet Model)

Calculate the cashflows of the mortgages assuming 100% PSA, 175% PSA, and 400% PSA. Graph the cashflows and balances.

Exercise 6-1d (Spreadsheet Model)

Compute the average life of the mortgages for 100% PSA, 175% PSA, and 400% PSA.

Work area

PSA	Average Life
100%	
175%	
400%	

Step 2 Create a Fixed-Rate Sequential CMO

Sequential bonds are formed using a principal payment rule. All principal payments go to the first bond until it is retired, then principal cashflows go to the next bond.

Figure 6-1

A Fixed-Rate Sequential CMO at 175% PSA

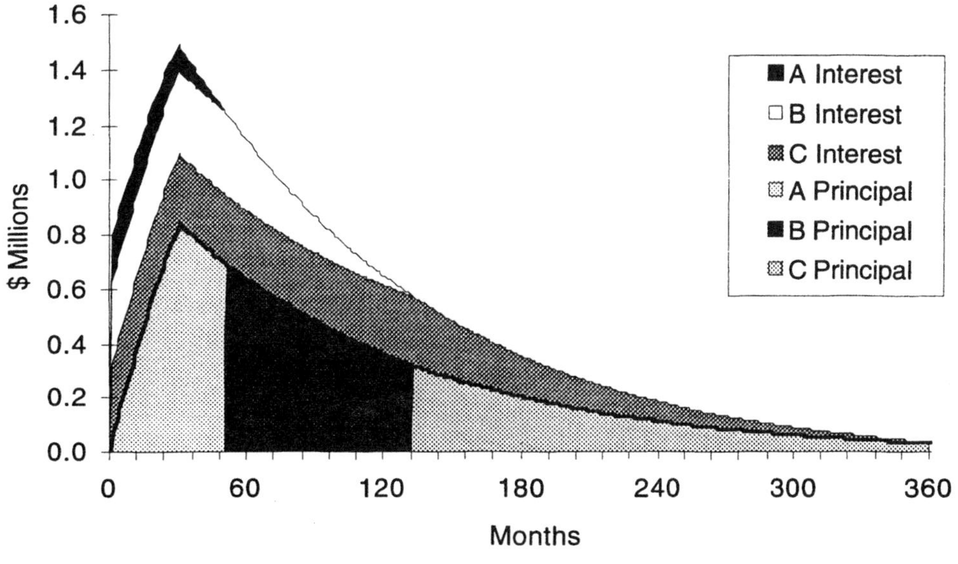

Fixed-rate is an interest payment rule. Each bond receives an interest payment each period equal to its beginning of period balance times its coupon. Even if the bond is not receiving a principal payment, it still receives interest payments. In the following exercise, there will be interest payments from the collateral that are not distributed to any bond. The cashflows for the fixed-rate sequential CMO to be built in Exercise 6-2c are shown in Figure 6-1.

Exercise 6-2

Start with the assumptions of Step 1. Assume the following bond characteristics:

Bond	Balance	Coupon
A	$30mm	7
B	$40mm	9
C	$30mm	10

Exercise 6-2a (Simple CMO Model)

Calculate the cashflows of bonds A, B, and C assuming 20% APP.

Exercise 6-2b (Simple CMO Model)

Calculate the average life of bonds A, B, and C assuming 20% APP.

Work area

Bond A

Year	Balance	Principal	Interest	Cashflow
1	30.0			
2				
3				
4				
5				
6				
Avg Life				

Bond B

Year	Balance	Principal	Interest	Cashflow
1	40.0	0	3.6	3.6
2				
3				
4				
5				
6				
Avg Life				

Bond C

Year	Balance	Principal	Interest	Cashflow
1	30.0	0		
2				
3				
4				
5				
6				
Avg Life				

Exercise 6-2c (Spreadsheet Model)

Calculate and graph the cashflows of bonds A, B, and C assuming 175% PSA.

Exercise 6-2d (Spreadsheet Model)

Calculate the average life of bonds A, B, and C assuming 175% PSA.

Work Area

Bond	Average Life
A	
B	
C	

■ REVIEW QUESTION (Advanced)

Write principal payment and interest payment rules that would produce a bond with the cashflows equal to the difference between the collateral cashflows and the bond cashflows.

Step 3 Create a Sequential CMO with a Z-Bond

A Z-bond or accrual bond is a principal pay rule. The Z bond does not receive any cashflow until the prior bonds are completely paid down. The interest due to the Z-bond, while the prior bonds are outstanding, is added (accrues) to the principal amount due to the Z-bond. That cashflow is then added to the principal available to pay down the prior bonds. In other words, the accrual structure converts the interest accruing to the Z-bond into principal for payment to other bonds. Once the other bonds are retired, the Z-bond pays interest and principal currently. Figure 6-2 shows the cashflows of the sequential CMO with a Z-bond as calculated in Exercise 6-3c.

Figure 6-2

Sequential with a Z-bond at 175% PSA

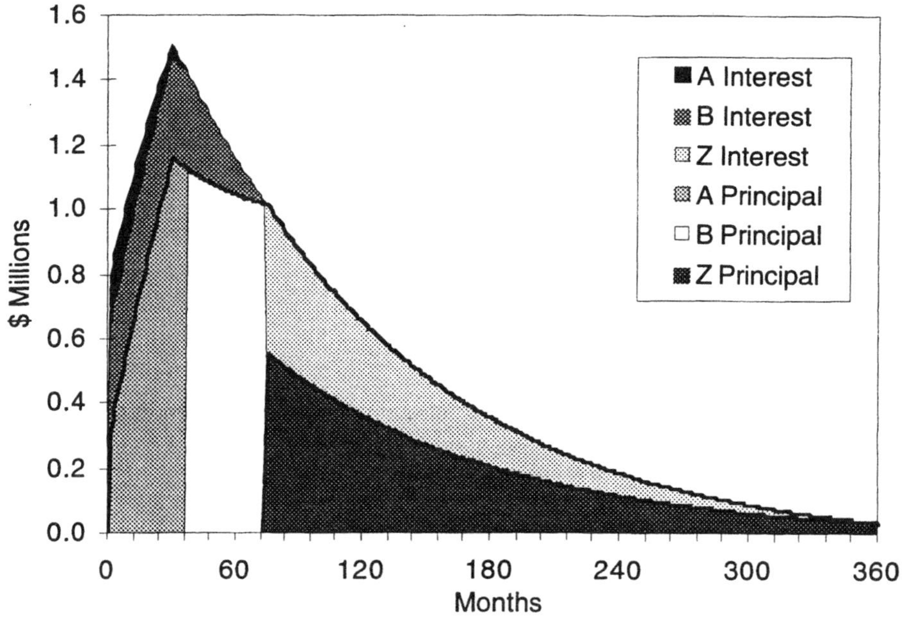

Exercise 6-3

Replace bond C above with bond Z, an accrual bond.

Exercise 6-3a (Simple CMO Model)

Calculate the cashflows of bonds A, B, and Z assuming 20% APP.

Bond	Balance	Coupon
A	30.0	7
B	40.0	9
Z	30.0	10

Work area

Bond A

Year	Balance	Principal	Interest	Cashflow
1	30.0			
2				
3				
4				
5				
6				

Bond B

Year	Balance	Principal	Interest	Cashflow
1	40.0			
2				
3				
4				
5				
6				

Bond Z

Year	Balance	Principal	Interest	Accrual	Cashflow	Net Principal
1	30.0	0.0	3.0	–3.0	0	–3.0
2						
3						
4						
5						
6						

Exercise 6-3b (Simple CMO Model)

Calculate the average life of bonds A and B assuming 20% APP. Compare these to the average lives calculated in Step 2.

Work area

Bond	Average Life No Z	Average Life W/Z
A		
B		

Exercise 6-3c (Spreadsheet Model)

Calculate and graph the cashflows of bonds A, B, and Z assuming 175% PSA.

Exercise 6-3d (Spreadsheet Model)

Calculate the average life of bonds A and B assuming 175% PSA. Compare these to the average lives calculated in Step 2.

Work area

Bond	Average Life No Z	Average Life W/Z
A		
B		

Exercise 6-3e (Advanced)

Calculate the average life of the Z bond in Exercise 6-3c. Accruals create negative principal cashflows. How does this impact the calculations of average life?

Work area

Bond	Average Life
Z	

Step 4 Create a Pro-Rata CMO

Pro-rata is a principal pay rule. It is primarily used to assign different coupons to bonds with the same principal payment characteristics. Pro-rata bonds receive principal payments in fixed proportion to each other. They can be created by splitting cashflows of a bond. Figure 6-3 shows a pro-rata bond created from Bond B of Figure 6-1 as created in Exercise 6-4c.

Figure 6-3
A Pro-Rata Bond

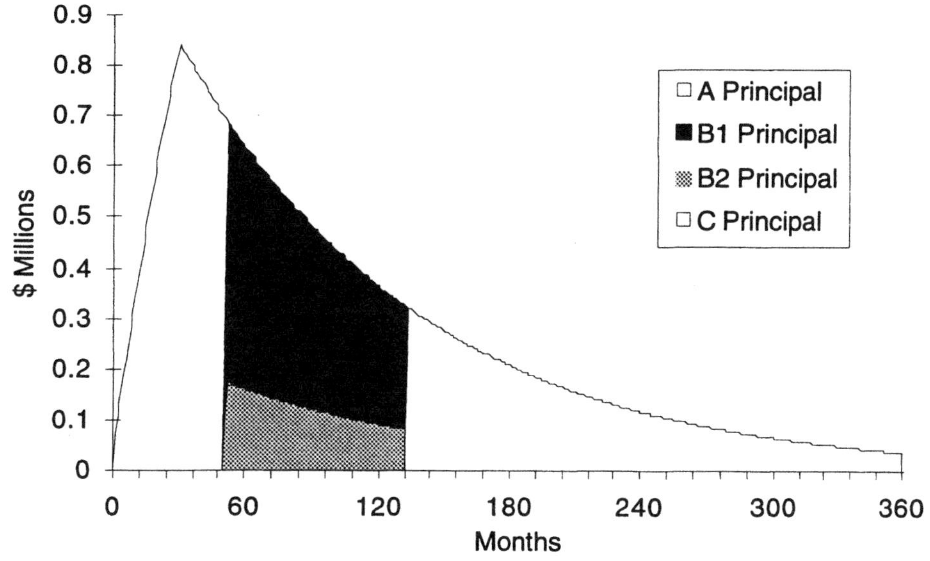

This is an example of the layering technique. The pro-rata structure is usually applied to a set of cashflows created through one of the other structuring methods.

The total interest payments of the pro-rata bonds must be less than or equal to the interest payments of the underlying bond. It is possible to have a pro-rata class that does not receive any principal or a class that does not receive any interest. (See IO/PO structuring in Step 7.)

Exercise 6-4

Create pro-rata bonds using Class B created in Step 2 (without the Z bond). Assume Class B1 receives 75% of the principal payments of Bond B. Assume Class B2 receives 25% of the principal payments of Bond B.

Exercise 6-4a (Simple CMO Model)

Assume that the coupon on Bond B1 is 8%. What is the maximum coupon on bond B2?

Exercise 6-4b (Simple CMO Model)

Compute and graph the cashflows of bonds B1 and B2 using the maximum coupon for bond B2. Use 20% APP.

Work area

Pro-Rata

Bond	Share	Coupon
B1	75%	8
B2	25%	

	Principal		Interest	
Year	**B1**	**B2**	**B1**	**B2**
1	0.00	0.00	2.40	1.20
2	7.50	2.50	2.40	1.20
3				
4				
5				
6				
Total	30.00	10.00	7.20	3.60

Exercise 6-4c

Compute and graph the cashflows of bonds B1 and B2 assuming 175% PSA.

Step 5 Create Floater/Inverse Floater Coupons

Floaters and inverse floaters are interest pay rules. Floating rate coupons are set at a margin above an index. There is also a cap and a floor on the coupon rate. A variety of indices are possible (subject to REMIC restrictions). LIBOR and Constant Maturity Treasury (CMT) indices are the most common.

Inverse floating coupons are set based on a formula so that the coupon decreases as LIBOR increases. The coupon is expressed as a base rate less the index times a multiple. The coupon has a floor that may be zero or higher.

Exercise 6-5

Assume a pro-rata structure where the floater receives 75% of the principal payments, the underlying coupon is 9%, the floater is indexed to LIBOR with a 1% margin, and the other bond is an inverse floater.

Exercise 6-5a

What is the maximum cap on the floater? (Hint: Minimum inverse coupon is 0.)

Exercise 6-5b

What is the maximum coupon on the inverse floater? (Hint: Minimum floater coupon is equal to the margin.)

Exercise 6-5c

What is the multiplier on the inverse floater? (Hint: If one changes the floater coupon by 1%, what happens to the inverse floater coupon?)

Exercise 6-5d

Write down formulas for the floater and inverse floater coupons.

Exercise 6-5e

Fill in the table which shows the coupons on the floater and inverse floater for various levels of LIBOR.

Work area

LIBOR	Floater	Inverse
3		
6	7.00	
9		6.00
12		
15		

Step 6 Create a PAC/Support CMO

Planned Amortization Class (PAC) is a principal pay rule. A support bond is always created in conjunction with the PAC class. A PAC is created so that its principal cashflows are fixed for a certain range of prepayment rates, called the PAC band.

The support bond absorbs the principal cashflows that exceed those scheduled to be paid to the PAC. The PAC structure provides for a reallocation of prepayment risk. For this exercise we will return to the unstructured cashflows of Step 1. PAC cashflows are shown in Figure 6-4 for Exercise 6-6f.

Figure 6-4
PAC Cashflows at 175%

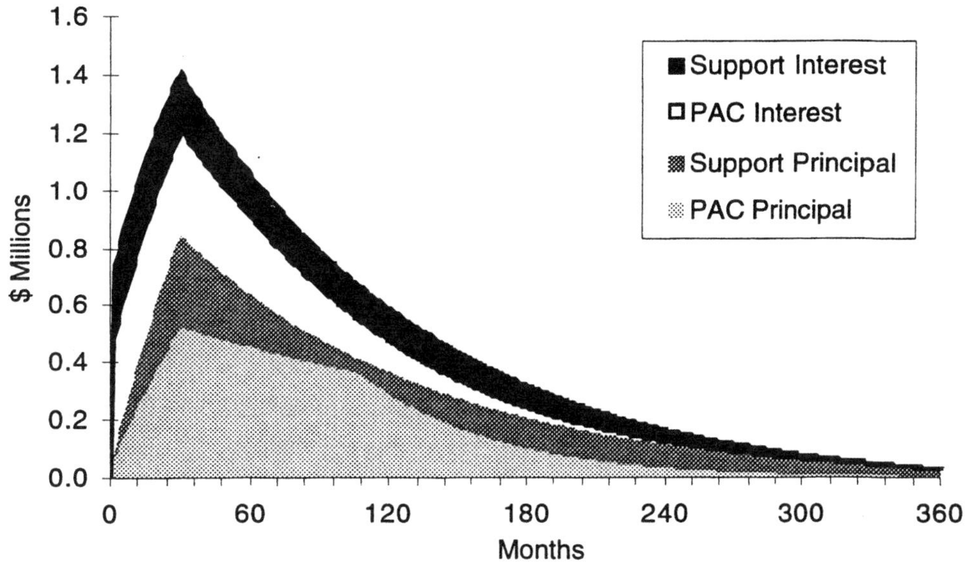

Exercise 6-6

Exercise 6-6a (Simple CMO Model)

Using the assumptions of Step 1, calculate the principal cashflows using a 10% APP and a 30% APP. (Note: These results are available in Exercise 6-1a.)

Exercise 6-6b (Simple CMO Model)

Use the smaller of the two principal payments for each period to determine the PAC schedule.

Exercise 6-6c (Simple CMO Model)

Add these principal payments to determine the PAC bond balance. Determine the scheduled balance for each period.

Work area

Year	Principal	Bands 10%	Bands 30%	PAC Schedule	Scheduled Balance
1	20.0	10			40
2	20.0		30		
3	20.0			10	
4	20.0				
5	20.0				
6	0.0				

	PAC		Support	
Year	Balance	Principal	Balance	Principal
1			60	
2				
3				10
4				
5				
6				

Exercise 6-6d (Simple CMO Model)

Calculate the principal cashflows of the PAC and support bonds assuming 5%, 10%, 30%, and 40% APP. Assume that principal payments will be made first to the PAC to pay down the PAC balance according to the PAC schedule. Excess principal will be used to reduce the principal balance of the support bond until its balance is reduced to zero. In the event of insufficient principal cashflow to meet the PAC schedule, the PAC has priority over the support bond for future payments until it has been paid down to its scheduled balance.

Exercise 6-6e (Simple CMO Model)

Calculate the average life of the bonds for 5%, 10%, 30%, and 40% APP.

Work area

		PAC Principal Cashflows			
Year	APP:	5%	10%	30%	40%
1					
2					
3					
4					
5					
6					
Avg life					

		Support Principal Cashflows			
Year	APP:	5%	10%	30%	40%
1					
2					
3					
4					
5					
6					
Avg life					

Exercise 6-6f (Spreadsheet Model)

Use 100% PSA and 300% PSA for the bands. Evaluate cashflows and average life at 75% PSA, 100% PSA, 175% PSA, 300% PSA, and 400% PSA.

Work area

	Average Life	
PSA	PAC	Support
75%		
100%		
175%		
300%		
400%		

■ REVIEW QUESTION (Advanced)

What happens if prepayments are 100% PSA for the first five years and then 300% PSA for the remaining time? What is the average life of the PAC bond? What if prepayments are 300% PSA for the first five years and then 100% PSA for the remaining time? Effective PAC bands represent the range of speeds for which the CMO will meet its schedule. How do they change over time?

Step 7 Create an IO and a PO

Interest Only (IO) and Principal Only (PO) are interest payment rules. IOs and POs are pro-rata bonds with different coupons. The coupon on the IO is based on a "notional" principal amount. That is, it does not receive any principal payments but the interest payment is calculated by multiplying the coupon times the balance of another class.

The simplest form of an IO and PO is to strip the entire MBS. In addition, any class can be separated into an IO and PO. An IO or PO can also be stripped out of any bond to raise or lower the coupon on the remaining bond.

Exercise 6-7

Take the mortgage of Step 1. Split the cashflows into principal and interest.

Assume that for the following scenarios the mortgages will have the following yields and prepayment rates.

Scenario	Yield	APP%	PSA
−1	7	40	600
base	8	30	400
+1	9	20	250
+2	10	10	125

Exercise 6-7a (Simple CMO Model)

For each yield level calculate the cashflows of the IO and PO using the appropriate prepayment rate. For each yield level calculate the price of the IO and PO. Compare these prices with the unstripped MBS for each scenario.

Exercise 6-7b (Simple CMO Model)

Calculate the effective duration, based on 100 basis point shifts, using the 8% yield scenario as the base case. (Note: Actually, IOs and POs would tend to have different yields.) See Chapter 7 for more information about effective duration.

Work area

Principal Only

	Yield	7%	8%	9%	10%
Year	**APP**	**40%**	**30%**	**20%**	**10%**
1					10
2		40			
3			30		
4				20	
5					
6					
	Price	$88.65			
	Effective Duration				

Interest Only

	Yield	7%	8%	9%	10%
Year	**APP**	**40%**	**30%**	**20%**	**10%**
1		10			
2				8	
3			4		
4					
5					6
6					
	Price				
	Effective Duration				

	Price Comparison			
	7%	**8%**	**9%**	**10%**
PO				
IO				
MBS				

■ REVIEW QUESTIONS (Advanced)

Compare the price profile of the bond created in Exercise 6-2e with the IO. Create a 2% coupon IO strip from the PAC bond in Step 6. Compare price profiles.

Create a PO from the support bond in Step 6. Compare the price profile to the PO created in Step 7.

(Very Advanced)

Using current market levels, create a sequential structure within a PAC class and create a pro-rata floater, inverse floater within the support class. Determine spread levels at which the CMO would have greater value than the underlying MBS. Strip all bond coupons to produce bond prices below par. How much of the value of the deal is in IO and inverse floater classes?

■ ANALYZING A DEAL STRUCTURE

Most CMOs combine the principal and interest payment rules to create a multitude of different bonds from one pool of underlying cashflows. Table 6-1 shows a typical CMO bond in a typical descriptive format. This particular example was adapted from a screen on the Bloomberg.

Table 6-1
FNMA 1994-22 REMIC Summary

Dates			Underlying	
Original Amount:	540,000MM		100% FNCL	7.5% Net
Priced:	1/12/94		Orig	9/8/95
Dated:	mixed	**WAC:**	7.9210	7.9171
Settled:	2/28/94	**WAM:**	29y 3m	27y 4m
First Pay:	3/25/94	**CAGE:**	0y 8m	2y 3m
9/95 Amount:	479,635MM			

Prepayments			
Orig Speed:	300 PSA		
1 mo. Hist:	156 PSA		
	PAC	**SUP/PAC**	**SUP**
Original:	55.0%	24.8%	20.2%
Current:	52.2%	26.1%	21.7%

Deal Structure

Class	Description	Cpn	Std Mty	Size (000)	Factor 9/95	Cur FLUX	Orig. WAL	WAL @200	Collar Band	Collar As Of
A	PAC II	5.000	3/22	243,000	0.808	1.1	3.5	2.9	357-519	9/95
B	PAC II	5.000	12/22	21,600	1.000	3.5	7.9	6.6	130-516	9/95
C	PAC II	5.000	12/23	29,700	1.000	2.9	10.4	8.8	120-482	9/95
D	PAC II	5.000	1/24	2,700	1.000	2.1	13.8	12.2	72-479	9/95
FA	FLT +	6.475	1/24	74,250	0.938	2.1	2.0	11.5	No Band	9/95
SA	INV +	3.590	1/24	23,265	0.938	30.3	2.0	11.5	No Band	9/95
SB	INV +	7.500	1/24	13,860	0.938	24.0	2.0	11.5	No Band	9/95
E	PO, SCH (22)	0.000	1/24	22,275	0.938	19.4	2.0	11.5	No Band	9/95
F	FLT, SUP	7.075	1/24	60,750	0.951	7.4	10.5	20.8	No Band	9/95
S	INV, SUP	2.406	1/24	48,600	0.951	37.4	10.5	20.8	No Band	9/95
R	R, NPR	0.000	1/24	0	1.000	—	—	—	—	—

Source: Bloomberg Financial Markets, 1995.

Exercise 6-8

Analyze the deal structure shown in Table 6-1.

Exercise 6-8a

Which bonds are the PAC classes? What relevance is the "as of" date of the collar?

Exercise 6-8b

Identify the sequential structure.

Exercise 6-8c

Identify the support bonds.

Exercise 6-8d

Identify the pro-rata bonds. How are they related? High/low coupon? Inverse/floater?

Exercise 6-8e

Why is the original WAL different from "WAL@200"?

Looking at a descriptive screen such as the one shown in Table 6-1 is not a substitute for review of the prospectus. Below we include an excerpt from the prospectus for the same deal. Note how the cash allocation rules in the prospectus confirm the analysis performed by looking at the deal summary.

Excerpt from FNMA REMIC 1994-22 Prospectus

Principal Distribution Amount

Principal will be distributed monthly on the Certificates in an amount (the "Principal Distribution Amount") equal to the aggregate distributions of the principal concurrently made on the SMBS.

On each Distribution Date, the Principal Distribution Amount will be distributed as a principal of the Classes in the following order of priority:

i. sequentially, to the A, B, C, D Classes, in that order, until the principal balances thereof are reduced to their respective Planned Balances for such Distribution Date;

ii. concurrently, to the FA, SA, SB and E Classes, in proportion to their original principal balances (or 55.5555555556%, 17.4074074074%, 10.3703703703% and 16.6666666667%, respectively), until their respective Scheduled Balances for such Distribution Date;

iii. concurrently, to the F and S Classes, in proportion to their original principal balances (or 55.5555555556% and 44.4444444444%, respectively), until the balances thereof are reduced to zero;

iv. concurrently, to the FA, SA, SB and E Classes, in the proportions set forth in clause (ii) above, without regard to the Scheduled Balances and until the principal balances thereof are reduced to zero; and

v. sequentially, to the A, B, C, and D Classes, in that order, without regard to the Planned Balances and until the respective principal balances thereof are reduced to zero.

■ REVIEW QUESTIONS

What structuring process segments the cashflows into bonds with different average lives? What is the advantage of creating bonds with different average lives?

What cashflow, if any, is left over in Step 2? What is the advantage of having the bond coupons set below the collateral coupon? What are the disadvantages?

Where does the accrual principal on a Z bond come from?

If both bonds have the same average life, which has a higher price, an accrual bond with a yield of 10% or a zero coupon bond with a yield of 10%? Why?

With a positively sloped yield curve, how does using a Z bond affect the value of the previous classes?

If two bonds have the same average-life profile, what type of bonds are they?

How can you increase the size of the PAC bond? How does this affect the cashflows of the support bond?

What happens to the cap on the floater when the percent of floater increases?

What happens to the leverage of the inverse?

Describe an inverse floater as a bond and short-term funding.

How does increasing the slope of the inverse affect the risk of the bond?

What is the sign on the effective duration of an IO? Why?

Is the effective duration of a PO higher or lower than its cashflow duration?

Why?

■ ANSWERS TO EXERCISES

6-1a & 6-1b

Underlying Security	
Balance	100
Coupon	10
Maturity	5

APP	10%			
Year	**Balance**	**Principal**	**Interest**	**Cashflow**
1	100	10.0	10.0	20.0
2	90	10.0	9.0	19.0
3	80	10.0	8.0	18.0
4	70	10.0	7.0	17.0
5	60	60.0	6.0	66.0
6	0	0.0	0.0	0.0
Avg Life		4.0		

APP	20%			
Year	**Balance**	**Principal**	**Interest**	**Cashflow**
1	100	20.0	10.0	30.0
2	80	20.0	8.0	28.0
3	60	20.0	6.0	26.0
4	40	20.0	4.0	24.0
5	20	20.0	2.0	22.0
6	0	0.0	0.0	0.0
Avg Life		3.0		

APP	30%			
Year	**Balance**	**Principal**	**Interest**	**Cashflow**
1	100	30.0	10.0	40.0
2	70	30.0	7.0	37.0
3	40	30.0	4.0	34.0
4	10	10.0	1.0	11.0
5	0	0.0	0.0	0.0
6	0	0.0	0.0	0.0
Avg Life		2.2		

6-1c

Balance 100% PSA

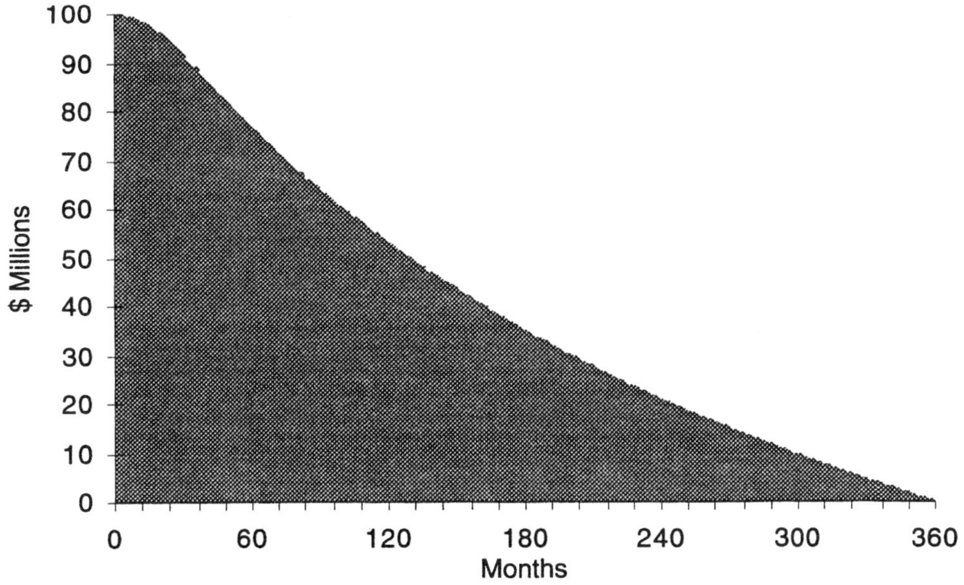

Cashflow 100% PSA

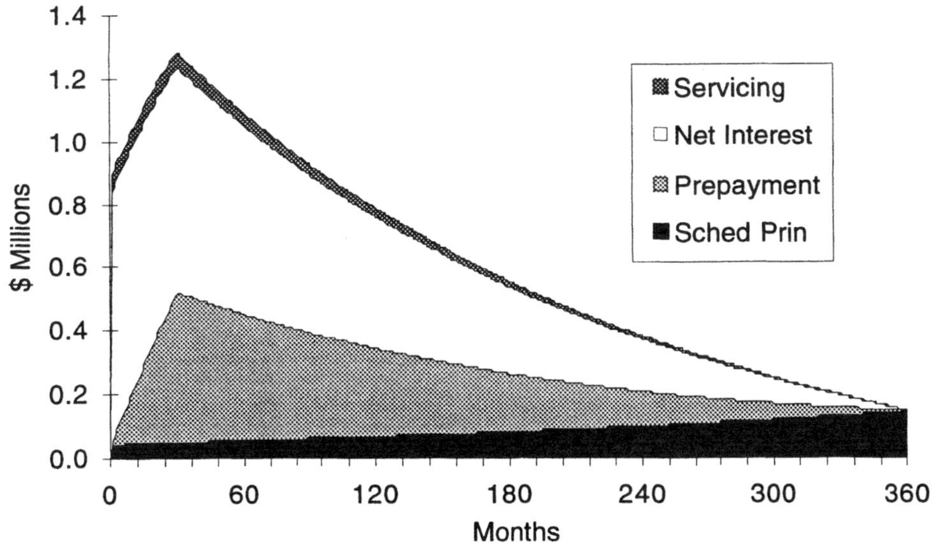

Balance 400% PSA

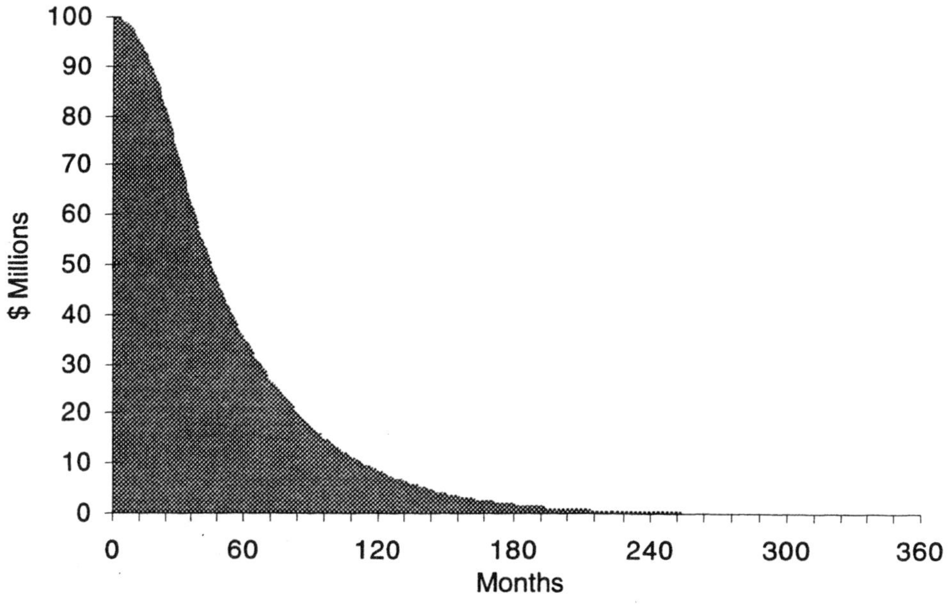

Cashflow 400% PSA

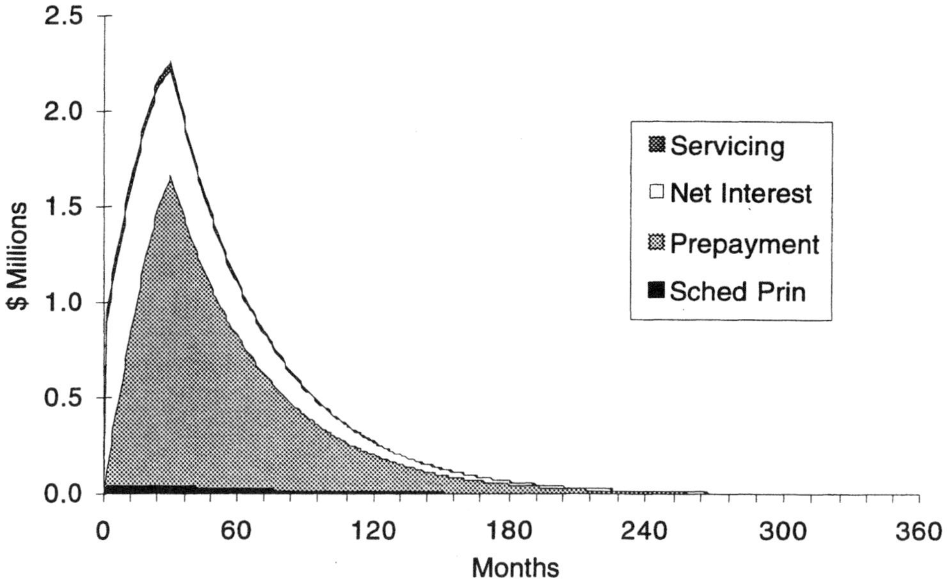

6-1d

PSA	Average Life
100%	12.40
175%	8.93
400%	4.75

6-2a, b

Sequential

Bond	Balance	Coupon
A	30.0	7
B	40.0	9
C	30.0	10
Total	100.0	

Bond A

Year	Balance	Principal	Interest	Cashflow
1	30.0	20.0	2.1	22.1
2	10.0	10.0	0.7	10.7
3	0.0	0.0	0.0	0.0
4	0.0	0.0	0.0	0.0
5	0.0	0.0	0.0	0.0
6	0.0	0.0	0.0	0.0
Avg Life		1.3		

Bond B

Year	Balance	Principal	Interest	Cashflow
1	40.0	0.0	3.6	3.6
2	40.0	10.0	3.6	13.6
3	30.0	20.0	2.7	22.7
4	10.0	10.0	0.9	10.9
5	0.0	0.0	0.0	0.0
6	0.0	0.0	0.0	0.0
Avg Life		3.0		

Bond C

Year	Balance	Principal	Interest	Cashflow
1	30.0	0.0	3.0	3.0
2	30.0	0.0	3.0	3.0
3	30.0	0.0	3.0	3.0
4	30.0	10.0	3.0	13.0
5	20.0	20.0	2.0	22.0
6	0.0	0.0	0.0	0.0
Avg Life		4.7		

6-2c

See Figure 6-1.

6-2d

Bond	Average Life
A	2.55
B	7.29
C	17.51

6-3a

Accrual

Bond	Balance	Coupon
A	30.0	7
B	40.0	9
Z	30.0	10

Bond A

	Balance	Principal	Interest	Cashflow
1	30.0	23.0	2.1	25.1
2	7.0	7.0	0.5	7.5
3	0.0	0.0	0.0	0.0
4	0.0	0.0	0.0	0.0
5	0.0	0.0	0.0	0.0
6	0.0	0.0	0.0	0.0
Avg Life		1.2		

Bond B

Balance	Principal	Interest	Cashflow
40.00	0.00	3.60	3.60
40.00	16.30	3.60	19.90
23.70	23.63	2.13	25.76
0.07	0.07	0.01	0.08
0.00	0.00	0.00	0.00
0.00	0.00	0.00	0.00
Avg Life	**2.6**		

Bond Z

Balance	Principal	Interest	Accrual	Cashflow	Net Principal
30.0	0.0	3.0	–3.0	0.0	–3.0
33.0	0.0	3.3	–3.3	0.0	–3.3
36.3	0.0	3.6	–3.6	0.0	–3.6
39.9	19.9	4.0	0.0	23.9	19.9
20.0	20.0	2.0	0.0	22.0	20.0
0.0	0.0	0.0	0.0	0.0	0.0
Avg Life	4.5				

6-3b

	Average Life	
Bond	**No Z**	**W/Z**
A	1.3	1.2
B	3.0	2.6

6-3c

See Figure 6-2.

6-3d

	Average Life	
Bond	**No Z**	**W/Z**
A	2.55	1.83
B	7.29	4.60

6-3e

Bond	Average Life
Z	21.79

The negative principal cashflows increase average life.

6-4a

The maximum coupon on Bond B2 is 12%.

6-4b

Pro-Rata

Bond	Share	Coupon
B1	75%	8%
B2	25%	12%

	Principal		Interest	
Year	B1	B2	B1	B2
1	0.0	0.0	2.40	1.20
2	7.5	2.5	2.40	1.20
3	15.0	5.0	1.80	0.90
4	7.5	2.5	0.60	0.30
5	0.0	0.0		
6	0.0	0.0		
Total	30.0	10.0	7.20	3.60

6-4c

See Figure 6-3.

6-5a

The maximum cap on the floater is 12%.

6-5b

The maximum coupon on the inverse floater is 33%.

6-5c

The multiplier on the inverse floater is 3.

6-5d

Floater Formulas:

Floater = Min(LIBOR +1%, 12%)

Inverse Floater = Max(33% – 3 × Libor, 0)

6-5e

LIBOR	Floater	Inverse
3	4	24
6	7	15
9	10	6
12	12	0
15	12	0

6-6a, b, c

PAC and Support

Year	Principal	Bands 10%	Bands 30%	PAC Schedule	Scheduled Balance
1	20	10	30	10	40
2	20	10	30	10	30
3	20	10	30	10	20
4	20	10	10	10	10
5	20	60	0	0	0
6	0	0	0	0	0

Year	PAC Balance	PAC Principal	Support Balance	Support Principal
1	40	10	60	10
2	30	10	50	10
3	20	10	40	10
4	10	10	30	10
5	0	0	20	20
6	0	0	0	0

6-6d, e

PAC Principal Cashflows					
Year	APP:	5%	10%	30%	40%
1		5	10	10	10
2		5	10	10	10
3		5	10	10	20
4		5	10	10	0
5		20	0	0	0
6		0	0	0	0
Avg life		3.75	2.50	2.50	2.25

Support Principal Cashflows					
Year	APP:	5%	10%	30%	40%
1		0	0	20	30
2		0	0	20	30
3		0	0	20	0
4		0	0	0	0
5		60	60	0	0
6		0	0	0	0
Avg life		5.00	5.00	2.00	1.50

6-6f

	Average Life	
PSA	PAC	Support
75%	8.65	23.12
100%	7.56	20.46
175%	7.56	11.23
300%	7.56	3.35
400%	6.17	2.38

6-7a, b

Principal Only

Year	Yield: APP:	7% 40%	8% 30%	9% 20%	10% 10%
1		40	30	20	10
2		40	30	20	10
3		20	30	20	10
4		0	10	20	10
5		0	0	20	60
6		0	0	0	0
	Price	$88.65	$84.66	$77.79	$68.95
	Effective Duration		6.4		

Interest Only

Year	Yield APP	7% 40%	8% 30%	9% 20%	10% 10%
1		10	10	10	10
2		6	7	8	9
3		2	4	6	8
4		0	1	4	7
5		0	0	2	6
6		0	0	0	0
	Price	$16.22	$19.17	$24.67	$31.05
	Effective Duration		–22.05		

Price Comparison

	7%	8%	9%	10%
PO	$88.65	$84.66	$77.79	$68.95
IO	$16.22	$19.17	$24.67	$31.05
MBS	$104.87	$103.83	$102.47	$100.00

Price Profile

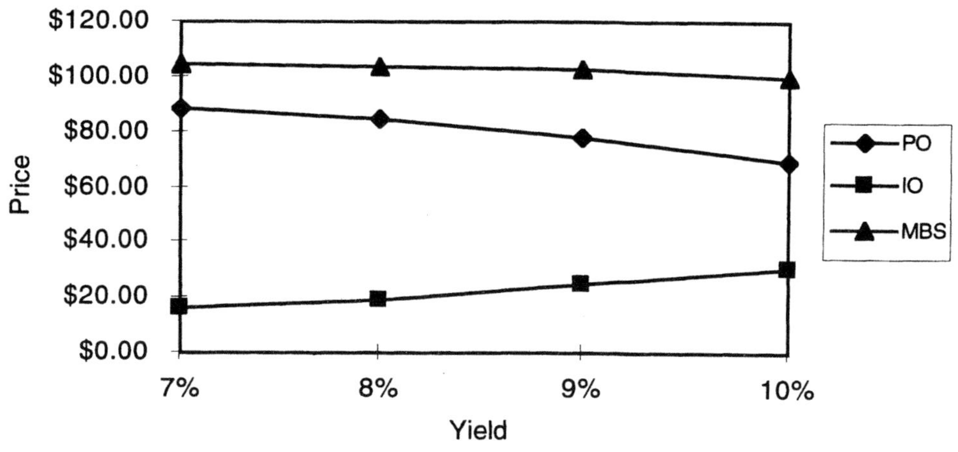

6-8a

Bonds A, B, C, and D are PAC classes. PAC collars shift as prepayment speeds change. The "band" is the effective collar for a particular date, calculated given the actual historical prepayments. A PAC collar can be "broken" if prepayment speeds go above or below the guidelines specified for the PAC. In this situation, investors will have reduced protection against cashflow variability due to prepayments.

6-8b

Bonds A, B, C, and D also represent a sequential structure within the PAC grouping. Note how the average life increases from Bond A to Bond D.

6-8c

All of the other bonds represent the support bonds for the PACs. They will be subject to more average life variability as prepayment rates change than the PAC bonds.

6-8d

The easiest way to spot pro-rata bonds is to find bonds with the same average life. If their average lives are the same under a variety of prepayment speeds they are very likely pro-rata bonds. Thus F and S are pro-rata bonds. They represent a floater/inverse floater combination. Also SA, SB, E and FA are a pro-rata combination with a more complex coupon interaction.

6-8e

The original WAL was calculated at 300% PSA. "WAL@200" indicates the current WAL calculated using the Andrew Davidson & Co., Inc. Prepayment Model for the scenario where rates rise by 200 basis points. At higher rates, prepayments slow. WAL increases as prepayments decrease.

CHAPTER SEVEN

Scenario Analysis

Susan continued to look over the investment proposal sent over from Bulls & Bears. The trade looked interesting, a recombination of an IO and PO off of FNMA 8s that looked 1/4 point cheaper than the collateral. "It's true," she said to one of her colleagues, "that the two securities aren't off the same trusts, but it looks like a good bet."

Susan spent some time trying to figure out what could go awry with the trade. Then she noticed that the WAC on the IO was .25% above the PO and that the same prepayment assumptions were being made in all the yield scenarios she was looking at. "What happens if the IO prepays differently than the PO in the yield scenarios?" she wondered. Using scenario analysis, she discovered that the combination underperformed collateral in a down 50 basis point scenario but only slightly outperformed when rates were rising 50 basis points. On balance, it looked like Bob from Bulls & Bears was up to his old tricks again.

■ INTRODUCTION

Previous sections have dealt with elements of static analysis and basics of MBS cashflows. We have been introduced to prepayments and factors affecting cashflows, and will now tie them together with an analytical tool called scenario analysis.

Table 7-1
Four-Step Process

Environment	Prepayments	Cashflows	Analysis
Holding Period	Static	Interim	Value
Interest Rates	Vector	Terminal	Risk
Re-investment	Model	Income	
Scenario Creation			

This chapter deals with fundamentals of:

- Total return calculations.
- Varying cashflows by scenarios.
- Relationship between scenarios and MBS analysis.

The factors under consideration follow the general framework established in the book, as shown in Table 7-1.

We will proceed through the various topics in this chapter, leading the reader through the development of the various techniques employed with scenario analysis. By the end of the chapter we hope to have developed an understanding of how to create a simple scenario analysis and how critical assumptions affect the analysis.

Environment

In order to understand how the method of scenario analysis can be applied to MBS, we will build off the basic cashflow examples developed earlier. Scenario analysis differs from yield analysis because we must make some explicit assumption regarding a holding period. While yield examines the value from holding a security until the last cashflow, scenario analysis examines performance over a specific time period. The length of the period will influence the weight of various assumptions and the interpretation of the results. In addition, there are a variety of ways to form a scenario resulting from the manner in which rates are shifted and how interim cashflows are re-invested.

Prepayments

The prepayment assumption must mirror the choice of interest rate scenario. We could either rely upon a prepayment model or apply static prepayment forecasts based on a specific scenario. By a static forecast we could assume, for example, that if interest rates remained constant, an MBS would prepay at 150% PSA and if rates were to drop, the MBS would prepay at 250% PSA. This static forecast would then be used for the entire life of the security.

Applying a prepayment model in the falling rate scenario would allow the prepayments to rise, but there would be additional fluctuations in prepayment rates due to seasonality, aging, and burnout. Prepayment models are considerably more useful when analyzing nonparallel yield curve shifts and when examining paths of interest rates.

Cashflows

Combining the change in interest rates with prepayment rates provides the information needed to project cashflows for the MBS. There are three general types of cashflows that will affect the total returns for securities: interim principal and interest, value of the remaining principal at the horizon, and income on the interim cashflows.

Analysis

Through examining the environment, prepayments, and cashflows, we build the various cashflow components of the scenario analysis. With the analysis methods we can put the pieces together and create some summary measures of performance and risk. These summary measures give an indication of both the absolute behavior of an MBS and provide a means to compare the relative performance of different securities.

In order to make matters somewhat more coherent, we introduce the concept of total return first. Having an understanding of the basic calculation will be important when examining the various factors that affect the measure.

■ COMPONENTS OF ENVIRONMENT

Total Return

Total rate of return (TRR) represents the basic measurement of value for scenario analysis. The TRR calculation compares the investor's final balance of cash against his starting balance. A growth rate is calculated to infer how the beginning balance could result in the ending balance.

This growth rate represents the overall cumulative gain and ignores the time of the holding period. The growth rate will generally be calculated as an annualized equivalent rate. Holding periods that are different than 12 months will require some normalization of the rate to place it on an annual basis.

Computation of Total Return

Assume we purchase a semi-annual coupon-bearing bond with a 5.9126% coupon at a price of par. At the end of six months, we receive a semi-annual coupon and we sell the bond at par. The total return computation is shown in Equation 7-1.

$$\text{6M TRR} = \frac{\text{Coupon} + \text{Terminal Value}}{\text{Starting Value}} - 1$$

$$= \frac{\$2.9563 + \$100}{\$100} - 1$$

$$= 2.9563\%$$

Equation 7-1
Total Return for a Six-Month Holding Period

Now, this is the total return assuming a six-month holding period. Normally we should put this into an annual equivalent. In our case, we would assume that the investor is able to put the money to work at the same rate for another six months. The annualized return is shown in Equation 7-2.

Equation 7-2
Annualized Total Return

$$
\begin{aligned}
\text{Annual TRR} &= \left(1 + \frac{\text{Six-month return}}{100}\right)^2 - 1 \\
&= \left(1 + \frac{2.9563}{100}\right)^2 - 1 \\
&= (1.0296)^2 - 1 \\
&= 0.06 \text{ or } 6\%
\end{aligned}
$$

Exercise 7-1

Using the same security as above, assume that the security is sold at the end of six months for a price of $101. Compute total return over the six-month period, then convert the six-month holding period return to an annual equivalent.

Holding Period

Choice of holding period length will play a role in scenario analysis because it can skew the manner in which results are interpreted. The shorter the holding period, the greater the effect of final price on the total rate of return. As the holding period lengthens, more weight gets placed on the assumed rate of re-investment.

In order to keep total rates of return on a comparable basis, we normalize returns to be quoted on an annual basis. Recall from Equation 7-2 that for a six-month holding period we compounded the results to get the annual equivalent. This compounding effect may lead to distorted results when the holding period is very short. For example, a $1 price increase that occurred over one day would lead to an extremely large annual total return.

Usually, scenario analysis considers a 12-month holding period to minimize any distortions. In the interest of brevity, however, most of the examples and exercises in this chapter use a six-month holding period.

Holding Period Length

Using the same 5.9126% coupon bond as in Exercise 7-1, let's assume that the security is held one year and then sold for a price of \$101. In this case, the total return would be as follows:

Total Return

$$= \frac{\text{Ending Cash}}{\text{Starting Cash}} - 1$$

$$= \frac{\text{Coupon Income}_{\text{Month 6}} + \text{Coupon Income}_{\text{Month 12}} + \text{Terminal Price}}{\text{Starting Price}} - 1$$

$$= \frac{2.9563 + 2.9563 + 101}{100} - 1$$

$$= \frac{106.913}{100} - 1$$

$$= 6.913\%$$

By moving the \$1 gain in terminal value from month 6 to month 12, we lose the effect of compounding the price increase. As a result, the total return on a 6-month basis exceeds the 12-month return (from Exercise 7-1) by more than 1%. Note that in the example above, we have ignored the effect of re-investing the coupon income received in month 6. The re-investment effect will be considered next.

Reinvestment Rate

The main computation in the total return metric is the comparison of the final cash balance to the starting balance. When considering final cash balance, we must make some assumption regarding the re-investment of cash received during the holding period. Depending upon the length of the holding period and the level of prepayments, this re-investment rate can play a material role in the total return computation.

Choosing a conservative re-investment rate is a good policy when evaluating the range of potential investments. This approach will tend to keep an investor from relying on unrealistic assumptions when projecting returns. Normally we make an assumption that cash received from a security will be re-invested at short-term money market rates. These rates should vary along with the scenario. For example, if we were looking at a scenario in which rates fell 100 basis points, the expected re-investment rate would also decline by 100 basis points in the scenario.

The Effect of Re-investment Rates

To illustrate the effect of re-investment rates, let's examine an MBS over a six-month holding period. The security has a gross WAC of 9%, net coupon of 8.5%, and WAM of 355. We will assume a 15% CPR and that cash will be invested in a risk free asset earning 6%.

Cash received in the first month will be re-invested for five months. Consequently, to determine the value at the end of six months of $1 received in month 1 we would use the formula shown in Equation 7-3.

Equation 7-3
Re-investment Rate Calculation

$$\left(1+\frac{6\%}{12}\right)^5 = 1.02525$$

To show the overall effect of re-investment, examine Table 7-2:

Table 7-2
Effect of Re-investment

Month	Balance	Interest	Principal	Re-investment	Interest w/Re-investment	Principal w/Re-investment
0	100.00					
1	98.60	0.71	1.40	1.02525	0.73	1.44
2	97.22	0.70	1.38	1.02015	0.71	1.41
3	95.85	0.69	1.36	1.01508	0.70	1.38
4	94.51	0.68	1.34	1.01003	0.69	1.36
5	93.18	0.67	1.33	1.00500	0.67	1.33
6	91.87	0.66	1.31	1.00000	0.66	1.31
Total		4.11	8.12		4.16	8.23

The columns show the basic interest and principal. In the fifth column we include the horizon value of each $1 of interest and principal. We are implicitly assuming that cashflows occur at the end of the period. In the last two columns the interest and principal amounts received are multiplied by the horizon values to get the horizon amounts. In Table 7-3, we compute the total returns with and without re-investment.

Table 7-3

Total Returns with and without Re-investment

	No Re-investment	With Re-investment
Purchase Price	100.00	100.00
Horizon Price	102.00	102.00
Horizon Balance	91.87	91.87
Principal Terminal Value	93.71	93.71
Coupon Income	4.10	4.16
Principal Returned	8.13	8.23
Ending Cash	105.94	106.10
Total Return (annualized)	12.24%	12.57%

Reinvestment only adds $0.16 in additional income but this translates into 0.33% in total return.

Exercise 7-2

Using the data in Table 7-2 and 7-3, compute the total return assuming that we earn 8% from re-invested principal and interest.

Work area

Terminal	
Coupon	
Principal Returned	
Ending Cash	
Total Return (annualized)	

Exercise 7-3

Using the same security as Exercise 7-1, assume that the coupon payment received in month 6 is re-invested at an annual rate of 6% for six months. Continue to assume a horizon price of $101. What is the resulting total rate of return?

Scenarios

The scenario itself represents the essence of the scenario analysis method. Someone employing the method can adopt several approaches to examine the sensitivity of MBS to a variety of potential scenarios. Common methods to create scenarios include:

Parallel Shifts Changes in the term structure translate into parallel movements in yields. That is, rates shift by an equal number of basis points across the curve. These parallel movements can be associated with probabilities in order to weight the scenarios and calculate an expected return.

Nonparallel Shifts Allow for shifts in the shape of the yield curve. These nonparallel shifts can be used to judge effects such as flattenings, inversions, and steepenings of the yield curve.

Paths/Whipsaw Shifts Instead of trying to average returns over a variety of scenarios it may be more useful to examine the sensitivity to particular paths of rates. In a whipsaw scenario one could specify a future scenario where rates oscillated and then flattened out at a long-term level.

■ COMPONENTS OF CASHFLOWS

Interim Cashflows

Interim cashflows, represented by the principal and interest, will be governed by the characteristics of the security, such as the coupon and WAM, as well as the prepayments estimated for a particular scenario. We can derive interim cashflows for a scenario using the methods developed in previous chapters.

Assume an MBS with a gross coupon of 9%, net coupon of 8.5%, and a WAM of 355. Let's consider a scenario in which the prepayment rate remains constant at 15% CPR. Also, assume that the starting balance of the MBS is $1,000. The cashflows are shown in Table 7-4.

Table 7-4
Cashflows for 8.5% MBS at 15% CPR

Month	Balance	Amortized Principal	Prepaid Principal	Interest	Servicing	Investor Cashflow	CPR
0	1,000.00						
1	985.99	0.57	13.44	7.08	0.42	21.10	15%
2	972.17	0.57	13.26	6.98	0.41	20.81	15%
3	958.53	0.56	13.07	6.89	0.41	20.52	15%
4	945.09	0.56	12.89	6.79	0.40	20.23	15%
5	931.83	0.55	12.71	6.69	0.39	19.96	15%
6	918.75	0.55	12.53	6.60	0.39	19.68	15%

Exercise 7-4

Rising Prepayment Rates

Instead of having prepayment rates flat at 15% CPR, now assume prepayment rates rise 5% CPR per month starting in month 2 and continuing until month 6. Recreate the cashflows from Table 7-4.

Work area

Month	Balance	Amortized Principal	Prepaid Principal	Interest	Servicing	Investor Cashflow	CPR
0	1,000.00						
1							15%
2							20%
3							25%
4							30%
5							35%
6							40%

Terminal Value

At the end of a specific holding period, the investor has three basic types of funds: cash received from interim principal and interest, reinvestment income on the principal and interest, and the remaining value of the principal. This remaining value depends upon both the price and the remaining balance. Thus, an investor must be cognizant of the relationship between prepayment rates and terminal value.

Consider scenarios of falling rates. Higher prepayment rates will occur along with rising prices. However, the high prepayment rates experienced during the scenario lead to less remaining principal. As a result, the MBS investor does not benefit as fully from price appreciation due to falling interest rates as an investor in a nonamortizing security.

Another consideration is the method used to determine the price of a security at the horizon. Generally, the choice will be between a static method or an OAS-based method. In a static method some assumption must be made regarding the yield spread of an MBS relative to some benchmark. For example, pricing the MBS at some fixed number of basis points over an equivalent average life Treasury.

When using an OAS-based method the following procedure is usually followed:

1. Compute the OAS based on current market levels.
2. Project cashflows for the scenario.

3. Use the horizon yield curve to compute the price based upon the starting OAS.

OAS will be discussed in more detail in Chapter 9.

Exercise 7-5

Using the cashflows from Table 7-4 and assuming a starting balance of $1,000 compute the missing numbers in the following table. Use the first column, which assumes a terminal price of $95 as an example.

Work area

	Base Case	Case 1	Case 2
Starting Price	100.00	100.00	100.00
Terminal Price	95.00	100.00	110.00
Terminal Balance	918.75	918.75	918.75
Terminal Value	872.81		
Coupon Income	41.04	41.04	41.04
Principal Returned	81.25	81.25	81.25
Ending Cash	995.10		
Total Return (semi-annual)	–0.49%		
Total Return (annualized)	–0.98%		

Income

During the holding period, the investor benefits from the coupon income received. Coupon flows will be classified as the income component of a total rate of return. The income component will also be affected by prepayments—the greater the prepayment rate the less underlying collateral to provide coupon income. In addition, for floating rate MBS the income will be dependent on the reset levels of the coupon.

Coupon Income

Let's return to our basic cashflow example. Consider an 8.5% MBS with a gross coupon of 9% and a WAM of 355. Assuming a 15% CPR over the period, the coupon interest and servicing for the first six months have been calculated and displayed in Table 7-5.

The interest for the first period equals (8.5/1200) × 1,000 or 7.08. In each succeeding period we compute the interest on the outstanding balance for the beginning of the period. The servicing cashflow is calculated from the 50 basis point difference between the gross and net coupons.

Table 7-5
Cashflows for an 8.5% MBS at 15% CPR

Month	Balance	Interest	Servicing
0	1,000		
1	985.99	7.08	0.42
2	972.17	6.98	0.41
3	958.53	6.89	0.41
4	945.09	6.79	0.40
5	931.83	6.69	0.39
6	918.75	6.60	0.39

Exercise 7-6

Using the indicatives in the example above, compute the total interest received by the investor under cases of 5% and 20% CPR. You will want to re-use the cashflow calculator built for Exercise 7-4.

Work area

Month	15% CPR Interest	5% CPR Interest	20% CPR Interest
1	7.08		
2	6.98		
3	6.89		
4	6.79		
5	6.69		
6	6.60		
Total	41.04		

■ EFFECT OF CHANGING PREPAYMENT RATES ON TOTAL RETURN

In addition to the normal complexities of computing the total return, we must grapple with the effects of prepayment rates on the MBS. To illustrate the effects of prepayments and the relation to total return, let's consider our 8.5% MBS example. In Tables 7-6 and 7-7, we'll show the cashflows under two scenarios, 5% CPR and 15% CPR, and examine the influence on total return in Table 7-8.

Table 7-6
Cashflows with 5% CPR

Month	Balance	Interest	Principal
0	1,000.00		
1	995.17	7.08	4.83
2	990.36	7.05	4.81
3	985.56	7.02	4.79
4	980.79	6.98	4.78
5	976.03	6.95	4.76
6	971.29	6.91	4.74
		41.99	28.71

Table 7-7
Cashflows at 15% CPR

Month	Balance	Interest	Principal
0	1,000.00		
1	985.99	7.08	14.01
2	972.17	6.98	13.82
3	958.53	6.89	13.63
4	945.09	6.79	13.44
5	931.83	6.69	13.26
6	918.75	6.60	13.08
		41.04	81.25

Table 7-8
Total Return

	5% CPR	15% CPR
Terminal Balance	971.29	918.75
Terminal Price	100.00	100.00
Terminal Value	971.29	918.75
Coupon	41.99	41.04
Principal Returned	28.71	81.25
Ending Cash	1,041.99	1,041.04
Total Return (semi-annual)	4.20%	4.10%
Total Return (annualized)	8.57%	8.38%

When prepayment rates increase we receive less coupon income, usually leading to a lower total return. However, when we have situations where the coupon is lower than the reinvestment rate, the previous generalization may not hold true. In addition, the example makes a simplifying assumption that holds the horizon price constant in both scenarios. We would normally expect the price in the 15% CPR scenario to be higher, causing the total return to increase.

Exercise 7-7

Using the data from Table 7-2 change the prepayment rate to 40% CPR. Using the cashflow table below, fill in the various components of total return.

Month	Balance	Interest	Principal
0	100.00		
1	95.78	0.71	4.22
2	91.73	0.68	4.04
3	87.86	0.65	3.87
4	84.15	0.62	3.71
5	80.59	0.60	3.55
6	77.19	0.57	3.40

Work area

Horizon Price	105.00	106.00
Terminal Value		
Coupon		
Principal Returned		
Ending Cash		
Total Return (annualized)		

■ COMPARING MBS AND TREASURY TRR

We can now tie some concepts together through a comparison of MBS and Treasury total rates of return. This will help to show how the interaction of prepayment rates and terminal pricing assumptions plays a large role in affecting the relative returns between securities.

For the comparison, six-month total returns were calculated for a FNMA 8% 30-year MBS and the five-year on-the-run Treasury. Parallel shifts of the yield curve from +300 to –300 basis points were considered. The FNMA 8% had an initial price of 102-12. In addition to the total returns, the terminal prices of the MBS and its average life have been calculated. Total returns were calculated using the TRA function on the Bloomberg.

Table 7-9
Total Return for Different Scenarios

Scenario	TRR MBS	TRR 5-Year Treasury	MBS WAL	MBS Terminal Price
–300	12.57	29.97	1.64	105.16
–200	9.70	21.58	1.64	103.59
–100	8.21	13.57	2.16	102.73
0	7.47	5.92	6.51	102.24
100	–2.32	–1.39	9.83	97.10
200	–12.83	–8.38	10.46	91.60
300	–22.68	–15.06	10.87	86.44

In the unchanged yield curve case, the MBS has a significant total-return advantage over the Treasury. However, as the yield curve shifts we see significant divergence between the MBS and the Treasury. When rates fall, the MBS has a lower total return and when rates rise the performance of the MBS is also worse than the Treasury. This result is related to the negative convexity of the MBS, which will be explored in greater detail in the following section.

To understand the behavior of the MBS we must consider the role of prepayments and total return. As interest rates drop, accelerating prepayment rates keep the price of the MBS from rising very much. On the other side, as rates rise the extension of the average life causes the price to decline more than expected.

The underperformance of the MBS is also related to the manner in which terminal prices are determined. The total return example prices the MBS relative to the yield of the interpolated average-life Treasury. As we move out on the yield curve the benchmark yield rises. As interest rates fall investors are likely to widen the expected yield spread between the MBS and the Treasury benchmark.

■ RISK MEASURES

While an investment will normally be evaluated on a total return basis, some consideration must be made regarding the interim price risk of a security. The road is littered with MBS investment crackups in which the investment manager made an investment in a high yielding security and was subsequently wiped out before realizing the expected yields. These situations occur because of extreme price sensitivity to changes in interest rates and other environmental factors.

The common risk measures used to examine fixed-income securities are duration and convexity as briefly described in Chapters 3 and 4. These measures are important because they can be used to determine the approximate price change of a security for a given change in yield (which we term Δyield). This equation, called the Taylor series expansion, is as follows:

Equation 7-4
The Taylor Series Expansion for a Percentage Price Change

$$\text{Percentage Price Change} = \text{Duration} \times \Delta\text{Yield} + 0.5 \times \text{Convexity} \times \Delta\text{Yield}^2 + \text{Higher Order Terms}$$

The equation above assumes that we are using the option-adjusted effective modified duration and effective convexity. For most applications of the equation, we ignore the higher order terms beyond convexity.

Duration

We define duration as the percentage change in price for a basis point change in yield. Duration comes in many flavors—the one commonly used for MBS is the option-adjusted effective modified duration. The option-adjusted component implies that we consider the effects of changing prepayment rates and pricing assumptions as interest rates move. To compute the effective duration, the formula previously shown in Chapter 3, Equation 3-16, is commonly employed.

Equation 7-5
Effective Modified Duration

$$\text{Effective Modified Duration} = \frac{-100}{\text{Price}_{\text{Base}}} \times \frac{\text{Price}_{+\Delta\text{Yield Scenario}} - \text{Price}_{-\Delta\text{Yield Scenario}}}{2 \times \Delta\text{Yield}}$$

To employ the formula, we need to know the current price for a security, denoted by $\text{Price}_{\text{Base}}$. Then we consider some change in interest rates, ΔYield. This change in yield needs to be large enough to induce some change in the expected prepayment rates. Usually shifts of 25 or 50 basis points are used.

The numerator in the equation contains the prices in the up and down shift scenarios. In many cases an OAS model will be used to project the prices. Using the base case price, an OAS will be calculated. The yield curve will then be shifted up and down, and the new value will be calculated using the OAS from the base case.

In the absence of an OAS model it would be acceptable to change the prepayment model and to modify the yield spread. Some investors use a simpler, yet effective method called the empirical duration. They derive the shifted prices by examining current market prices. For example, an 8% MBS would trade with a similar price as an 8.5% MBS in a down 50 basis point shift and like a 7.5% in an up 50 basis point shift.

Computing the Effective Duration

An example of the effective duration calculation is as follows:

$$\text{Price}_{\text{Base}} = 99.906$$

$$\Delta\text{Yield} = 50 \text{ basis points}$$

$$\text{Price}_{-\Delta\text{Yield}} = 102.127$$

$$\text{Price}_{+\Delta\text{Yield}} = 97.393$$

$$\text{Effective Duration} = \frac{-100}{99.906} \times \frac{97.393 - 102.127}{2 \times .50}$$

$$= 4.738\%$$

To interpret the effective duration we would say that, assuming convexity to be 0, if interest rates declined 100 basis points we would expect the price of the security to rise 4.738%. Strictly speaking, duration should be quoted as a negative number that reflects the inverse relationship between price and yield (IO securities excluded). The convention is to quote duration as a positive number and the terms in the duration equation have been arranged to give a positive result.

Exercise 7-8

Compute the effective duration for the securities in the following table.

Work area

	Bond 1	Bond 2	Bond 3
–50bp	55.83	105.19	23.03
Base	45.00	104.22	26.75
+50bp	36.38	103.03	29.92
Effective Duration			

Convexity

For most fixed-income securities the relationship between price and yield is not exactly linear, as shown in Chapter 4, Figure 4-8. The nonlinear aspect is termed convexity and most noncallable bonds have "positive" convexity. A security with "positive" convexity will experience prices rising at a greater rate than they fall for a corresponding change in interest rates. However, callable securities, such as MBS, have "negative" convexity. With a "negatively" convex security, the prices will rise less than they fall for a corresponding change in interest rates.

If we return to Equation 7-4, which approximates the price change for a change in yield, we see that the convexity is an additive term. When convexity is positive, the change in yield will result in higher prices when yields fall. In the case of a rising yield scenario, the effect of positive convexity will be to keep prices from falling further than would have been expected from the projected effect of duration. That is, positive convexity adds some buffer from a rising yield scenario (remember that we square the change in yield).

For securities with negative convexity we would see the opposite effect. When yields fall the convexity component results in a drag on price performance. However, when yields rise, prices fall at an accelerated rate.

Effective convexity is generally calculated as follows:

$$\text{Effective Convexity} = \frac{100}{\text{Price}_{\text{Base}}} \times \frac{\text{Price}_{+\Delta\text{Yield Scenario}} + \text{Price}_{-\Delta\text{Yield Scenario}} - 2 \times \text{Price}_{\text{Base}}}{\Delta\text{Yield}^2}$$

Equation 7-6
Effective Convexity

The multiplication by 100 is performed for scaling purposes.

Computing Effective Convexity

An example of the effective convexity calculation is as follows:

$\text{Price}_{\text{Base}} = 99.906$

$\Delta\text{Yield} = 50$ basis points

$\text{Price}_{-\Delta\text{Yield}} = 102.127$

$\text{Price}_{+\Delta\text{Yield}} = 97.393$

$$\text{Effective Convexity} = \frac{100}{99.906} \times \frac{97.393 + 102.127 - 2 \times 99.906}{0.5^2} = -1.169$$

Exercise 7-9

Using the prices from the previous exercise, compute the convexity of the three securities:

	Bond 1	Bond 2	Bond 3
–50bp	55.83	105.19	23.03
Base	45.00	104.22	26.75
+50bp	36.38	103.03	29.92
Convexity			

Estimating the Price Change

Now that we know the estimated duration and convexity, we can approximate the price change for a given parallel shift in the yield curve using Equation 7-4. Using our bond from the previous examples, let's project the percentage change in price for a 25 basis point decline in yield.

$$\text{Percentage Price Change} = \text{Duration} \times \Delta\text{Yield} + 0.5 \times \text{Convexity} \times \Delta\text{Yield}^2$$

$$= -4.738 \times (-0.25) + 0.5 \times (-1.169) \times (-0.25)^2$$

$$= 1.185 - 0.037$$

$$= 1.148$$

For a 25 basis point decline in rates, we would expect prices to increase by 1.148%. This would lead to the price rising from $99.906 to $101.053.

Exercise 7-10

Using the calculated durations and convexities compute the percentage price changes and the resulting prices for 25 and 100 basis point shifts in the yield curve for the three bonds in Exercises 7-8 and 7-9.

Work area

Price Change	Bond 1	Bond 2	Bond 3
25bp			
100bp			

Prices	Bond 1	Bond 2	Bond 3
25bp			
100bp			

■ REVIEW QUESTIONS

Suppose an investor were contemplating a purchase of an inverse floating rate bond. What would be the usefulness of examining a non-parallel shift in the yield curve?

Now assume that the stability of a PAC bond were being examined. How could a whipsaw scenario be used to track the stability of the security?

Why would one want to use a prepayment model to project prepayment rates in cases of changes in the shape of the yield curve?

■ ANSWERS TO EXERCISES

7-1

Semi-annual return = 3.96%

Annual equivalent return = 8.07%

7-2

Terminal	93.71
Coupon	4.17
Principal Returned	8.27
Ending Cash	106.15
Total Return (annualized)	12.68%

7-3

Total Rate of Return = 7%

7-4

Month	Balance	Amortized Principal	Prepaid Principal	Interest	Servicing	Investor Cashflow	CPR
0	1,000.00						
1	985.99	0.57	13.44	7.08	0.42	21.10	15%
2	967.27	0.57	18.15	6.98	0.41	25.70	20%
3	943.81	0.56	22.90	6.85	0.40	30.31	25%
4	915.63	0.55	27.62	6.69	0.39	34.86	30%
5	882.83	0.54	32.27	6.49	0.38	39.29	35%
6	845.54	0.52	36.77	6.25	0.37	43.55	40%

7-5

	Base Case	Case 1	Case 2
Starting Price	100.00	100.00	100.00
Terminal Price	95.00	100.00	110.00
Terminal Balance	918.75	918.75	918.75
Terminal Value	872.81	918.75	1,010.62
Coupon Income	41.04	41.04	41.04
Principal Returned	81.25	81.25	81.25
Ending Cash	995.10	1,041.04	1,132.91
Total Return (semi-annual)	–0.49%	4.10%	13.29%
Total Return (annualized)	–0.98%	8.38%	28.35%

7-6

Month	15% CPR Interest	5% CPR Interest	20% CPR Interest
1	7.08	7.08	7.08
2	6.98	7.05	6.95
3	6.89	7.02	6.82
4	6.79	6.98	6.69
5	6.69	6.95	6.56
6	6.60	6.91	6.44
Total	41.04	41.99	40.53

7-7

Horizon Price	105.00	106.00
Terminal Value	81.05	81.82
Coupon	3.83	3.83
Principal Returned	22.81	22.81
Ending Cash	107.6853	108.4572
Total Return (annualized)	15.96%	17.63%

7-8

	Bond 1	Bond 2	Bond 3
–50bp	55.83	105.19	23.03
Base	45.00	104.22	26.75
+50bp	36.38	103.03	29.92
Effective Duration	43.22	2.07	–25.76

7-9

	Bond 1	Bond 2	Bond 3
–50bp	55.83	105.19	23.03
Base	45.00	104.22	26.75
+50bp	36.38	103.03	29.92
Convexity	19.64	–0.84	–8.18

7-10

Price Change	Bond 1	Bond 2	Bond 3
25bp	11.42	0.49	–6.70
100bp	53.04	1.65	–29.85

Prices	Bond 1	Bond 2	Bond 3
25bp	50.14	104.73	24.96
100bp	68.87	105.94	18.77

CHAPTER EIGHT

The Yield Curve

"The timing looks right for a Fed easing and this bodes well for short average-life MBS," read the research report in Susan's hands. Yes, she had heard this story many times before but it always seemed to be built on some sort of spurious reasoning. If only she could develop some way to value the impact on MBS cashflows. Her single security calculators were just fine for yields and even vectors of prepayments, but they provided no guidance to judge the effect of a reshaped yield curve.

■ INTRODUCTION

In several previous chapters, we have concentrated on building tools related to both MBS and the yield curve. These tools have consisted of cashflow generators and methods of risk, and yield curve analysis. In this chapter, we bring some of these tools together to analyze the relationship between the yield curve and MBS value. The exercises in this chapter develop an understanding of how the entire curve relates to the MBS spread over Treasuries and how to relate curve reshaping to changes in value.

■ SHAPE OF THE CURVE

MBS have a fundamental relationship to the yield curve for several reasons. Monthly cashflows make the value of an MBS susceptible to changes in rates along the entire curve. While this is essentially true for all coupon-bearing securities, MBS will generally be affected more because cashflows are more "front loaded" than securities such as Treasury bonds. For example, changes in the short end of the yield curve are generally going to have a greater impact on the change in value for a 30-year MBS than for a 30-year Treasury bond.

The relationship between MBS cashflows and interest rates is well known. This has been the central focus of discussions related to prepayments. We will extend this relationship further to understand how expectations about forward rates influence MBS cashflow for purposes of valuation.

To get some feel for the impact of curve shape on prepayments and valuation, consider the upward sloping yield curve. An upward sloping yield curve indicates that the markets value securities as if rates are expected to increase in the future. If we used this rising rate scenario to drive a prepayment model, we would be slowing down the expected prepayment rates compared to an assumption of rates remaining constant at today's rates. Under the forward rate expectations, investors in premiums and IOs would benefit, while holders of discounts, POs, and inverse floaters would see an erosion of value. Forward rate expectations are built into valuation tools such as OAS, so it is important for an investor to understand the relationship between forward rates, cashflows, and valuation.

■ SPREAD TO THE BENCHMARK

MBS are essentially a spread product. That is, investors calibrate the relative advantage of an MBS to the Treasury yield curve to derive some measure of value. The Treasury curve serves as a useful benchmark because it both represents the risk-free rate of interest and has observable yields extending out to 30 years. Since other markets are compared to Treasuries, such as corporates and agencies, we can use the Treasury curve as a means to calibrate intermarket relative value.

The most common measure of spread compares the difference in yield between two securities. When comparing a five-year corporate issue to a five-year Treasury note, the comparison is somewhat straightforward. However, it makes no sense to compare the yield of a 30-year MBS to that of a 30-year Treasury. Although the two securities share a similar final maturity, the pattern and timing of cashflows do not make for a reasonable comparison.

The appropriate benchmark Treasury is chosen not based on the final maturity of an MBS but rather on its weighted average life (WAL).[1] The weighted average life is used as a proxy for the maturity of an MBS as it represents the average time to receipt of principal. In some cases, the Treasury benchmark is chosen by rounding the WAL of the particular MBS down to the closest on-the-run Treasury.

Spreads to Benchmark Treasury

Assume that the Treasury yield curve has the following rates:

[1] In some cases the benchmark spread may be compared to a Treasury of similar cashflow duration. In this way a benchmark is found that relates to the timing of both principal and interest.

Table 8-1
Sample Yield Curve

Maturity	Yield
1	4.50
2	5.00
3	5.75
5	6.00
10	6.60
30	7.00

We determine MBS spreads to a specific benchmark Treasury for the following securities:

Table 8-2
Spreads to Benchmark Treasury

	Yield	WAL	Benchmark Treasury	Spread (bps)
MBS 1	6.00	2.4	2	100
MBS 2	6.70	4.4	3	95
MBS 3	7.10	7.0	5	110
MBS 4	7.75	12.0	10	115

Exercise 8-1
Suppose you decide to relax the prepayment speeds somewhat on the MBS in the example above, just enough to push the WALs out a bit. Determine the appropriate benchmark by rounding (up or down) to the closest Treasury. Then compute the spread to the benchmark. For simplicity we'll hold the yields of the MBS constant.

Work area

	Yield	WAL	Benchmark Treasury	Spread (bps)
MBS 1	6.00	2.6		
MBS 2	6.70	4.6		
MBS 3	7.10	7.6		
MBS 4	7.75	12.8		

Spread to Interpolated Average Life

As the previous example and exercise illustrates, the interaction of prepayment assumption and choice of appropriate Treasury benchmark may be somewhat skewed. A small change in the prepayment assumption could lead to a very different picture regarding the spread of an MBS. In an upward sloping yield curve, MBS will be marketed with as much cashflow pushed to the front end of the yield curve as possible. This leads to an increase in the marketed spread of the security.

An alternative to the arbitrary choice of a benchmark is the use of the interpolated average-life Treasury. The average life of a coupon-bearing Treasury security is the same as its maturity. Consequently, we can compare the spread of an MBS with a 3.6-year average life by interpolating between the three- and five-year Treasury securities.

Using the securities in Table 8-2, we have interpolated the yield of the Treasury security with the same average life. Spreads are calculated relative to the interpolated Treasury instead of the specific benchmark.

Table 8-3

Spreads to Interpolated Treasury

	Yield	WAL	Benchmark Yield	Benchmark Spread
MBS 1	6.00	2.4	5.30	70
MBS 2	6.70	4.4	5.93	77
MBS 3	7.10	7.0	6.24	86
MBS 4	7.75	12.0	6.64	111

The greatest effect can be seen for the shorter MBS. This is consistent with the effects of the first exercise, which showed how spreads moved when we changed the benchmark security.

Exercise 8-2

Solve for the benchmark yield and interpolated spread for the securities in the table below, as shown in Table 8-3.

Work area

	Yield	WAL	Benchmark Yield	Benchmark Spread
MBS 1	6.00	2.6		
MBS 2	6.70	4.6		
MBS 3	7.10	7.6		
MBS 4	7.75	12.8		

■ SPREAD TO THE CURVE

Taking the spread to the interpolated average-life Treasury is a reasonable improvement over rounding to a specific Treasury but it still has its limitations. Most importantly, taking a spread to a point on the yield curve ignores the shape of the curve and the relationship to MBS valuation.

To point this out, let's recall the equation, shown in Chapter 3, used to calculate the yield of an MBS, as seen again in Equation 8-1.

$$\text{Price} = \frac{\text{Cashflow}_{T_1}}{(1+\text{Yield}/1200)^{T_1}} + \ldots + \frac{\text{Cashflow}_{T_{WAM}}}{(1+\text{Yield}/1200)^{T_{WAM}}}$$

$$\text{Price} = \sum_{i=1}^{WAM} \frac{\text{Cashflow}_{T_i}}{(1+\text{Yield}/1200)^{T_i}}$$

Equation 8-1
Price and Yield for an MBS

We solve for the yield that equates the present value of the cashflows to the current price (including accrued interest). The subscript T again refers to the time from settlement, including actual delay days.

Yield is a useful measure to capture the expected return from holding a security until its final cashflow but it makes a fairly significant assumption. Namely, solving for yield assumes that we can continually re-invest monthly cashflows at the yield of the security. This can be a fairly aggressive assumption for long dated securities with cashflows spread out along the yield curve. A more reasonable assumption would be to consider a constant re-investment rate above the Treasury curve. That is, solving for a constant spread instead of solving for a specific yield.

The spread we're going to solve for is a specified number of basis points above the zero coupon Treasury curve. This would lead to the following modification of Equation 8-1.

$$\text{Price} = \frac{\text{Cashflow}_{T_1}}{(1+S_{T_1}+\text{sprd})^{T_1}} + \ldots + \frac{\text{Cashflow}_{T_{WAM}}}{(1+S_{T_{WAM}}+\text{sprd})^{T_{WAM}}}$$

$$\text{Price} = \sum_{i=1}^{WAM} \frac{\text{Cashflow}_{T_i}}{(1+S_{T_i}+\text{sprd})^{T_i}}$$

Equation 8-2
Constant Spread over Zero Curve

In Equation 8-2, the S terms refer to the spot rates corresponding to the maturity of the MBS cashflow. That is, we discount the MBS cashflow occurring in month 24 by the 24-month spot rate. We solve for the constant spread over the spot rates that equates the present value of the cashflows to the current price of the MBS. The spot rates in Formula 8-2 have been converted to monthly equivalents for use with MBS.

Solving for Spot Rates and Spread

In Chapter 4, we developed the method for deriving the spot curve given a par curve. An example can be seen in Table 8-4.

Table 8-4
Par and Spot Yield Curves

Maturity	Par Rate	Spot Rate
1	5.0	5.000
2	6.5	6.549
3	8.0	8.168
4	9.0	9.294
5	9.5	9.862

In order to illustrate the calculation of spread, we will assume a security with the following annual cashflows, based on a 9.5% coupon, a price of par, and an arbitrary amortization schedule shown in Table 8-5.

Table 8-5
Cashflows for a 9.5% Bond

Year	Balance	Principal	Interest	Cashflow
0	100			–100
1	90	10	9.50	19.50
2	75	15	8.55	23.55
3	55	20	7.13	27.13
4	30	25	5.23	30.23
5	0	30	2.85	32.85

Solving for the constant spread would require us to solve the following equation:

Equation 8-3
Solving for Spread to the Curve

$$100 = \frac{19.5}{(1+.05+sprd)} + \frac{23.55}{(1+.06549+sprd)^2} + \ldots + \frac{32.85}{(1+.09862+sprd)^5}$$

We could solve the equation using a trial and error method or by using some more sophisticated techniques. Using the "Goal Seek" feature of Excel, we could solve the equation by finding the value of the spread that makes the sum of the cashflows minus the starting price of 100 equal to zero.

The results of solving for the spread and other measures are shown in Table 8-6, below:

Table 8-6
Spread Measures

WAL	3.5
Yield	9.50
Spread to WAL	100
Spread to Spot Curve	87

The yield of the security equals the coupon if the starting price equals par. The spread to the interpolated average life security equals 100 basis points. However, after adjusting to the entire curve, our spread equals 87 basis points. The spread to the zero curve is lower than to the weighted average life because of the curve's relative shape and the distribution of cashflows. The marginal rate of change in the spot curve increases relative to the par curve.

The cashflows and price from Table 8-5 have been modified as shown in Table 8-7:

Table 8-7
Modified Cashflows

Year	Balance	Principal	Interest	Cashflow
0	100			–102
1	70	30	9.50	39.50
2	45	25	6.65	31.65
3	25	20	4.28	24.28
4	10	15	2.38	17.38
5	0	10	0.95	10.95

Based on these values, the following yield and WAL were calculated:

WAL	2.50
Yield	8.55

Exercise 8-3a

What is the spread to the interpolated average life par yield curve?

Exercise 8-3b

Using a spreadsheet, you can solve for the spread to the curve using a numerical procedure. Otherwise, solve for the spread by interpolating through the following table:

Spread	Price Minus Discounted Cashflows
0	1.697
50	.621
75	.091
100	–.435

To solve for the spread to the curve find the point where the price minus the discounted cashflows goes to 0. (Hint: The spread will be between 75 and 100 basis points).

■ EFFECT OF CHANGING THE CURVE SHAPE

Now that we have constructed a method for calculating the spread to the curve, we can apply this measure to judge the impact of a curve reshaping. We can change the shape of the par curve and then revalue the security at the same constant spread to the curve. In Table 8-8, the change in the curve will come from a steepening. Rates on the short end are going to decline while we will hold rates on the long end constant.

Table 8-8
Revised Yield Curve

Maturity	Par Rate	Spot Rate
1	3.0	3.000
2	5.0	5.051
3	8.0	8.317
4	9.0	9.425
5	9.5	9.975

Table 8-9
Valuing Cashflows at Initial Zero Spread of 87 Basis Points

Year	Balance	Principal	Interest	Cashflow	Discount Factor	Discounted Cashflow
0	100			–100.00	1.0000	–100.00
1	90	10	9.50	19.50	0.9627	18.77
2	75	15	8.55	23.55	0.8913	20.99
3	55	20	7.13	27.13	0.7682	20.84
4	30	25	5.23	30.23	0.6757	20.42
5	0	30	2.85	32.85	0.5976	19.63

In Table 8-9, we have added two new columns: the discount factor and the discounted cashflow. The discount factors relate to the terms in Equation 8-2. For example, the discount factors can be computed as follows:

$$\text{Discount Factor}_1 = \frac{1}{(1+.03+.0087)} = 0.9627$$

$$\text{Discount Factor}_5 = \frac{1}{(1+.09975+.0087)^5} = 0.5976$$

Equation 8-4
Solving for Discount Factors

To determine the discounted cashflow, we multiply the discount factor times the cashflow. We can then sum the discounted cashflows to get the present value of the security. This is equivalent to using Equation 8-2, except that we have assumed annual, not monthly cashflows. After the steepening of the yield curve, the present value of the cashflows now equals $100.65. The effect of short rates falling was a rise in price.

The standard method of solving for present value as shown in Equation 8-1, does not reflect a change in the shape of the yield curve on value. Neither the numerator containing the cashflows nor the denominator containing the yield are allowed to change, so there is no way to approximate the change in value.

After shifting the price to $100.65 we recompute the following measures of spread:

Table 8-10

Spread Measures

WAL	3.5
Yield	9.27
Spread to WAL	77
Spread to Spot Curve	87

Exercise 8-4

Why did the measures of yield and spread to the WAL benchmark change after the yield curve steepened? Why does the WAL remain constant? Why does the spread to the spot curve now exceed the spread to the average life benchmark?

Exercise 8-5

Impact of an Inverted Curve

We can use the same methods developed in Table 8-4 to judge the impact of an inverted curve on value. Now we will assume the following curve shape:

Maturity	Par Rate	Spot Rate
1	11.0	11.000
2	10.0	9.950
3	9.5	9.420
4	9.0	8.874
5	8.0	7.746

We will use the same spread of 87 basis points to the curve to compute the value. In the table below, calculate the discount factors and discounted cashflows:

Work area

Year	Balance	Principal	Interest	Cashflow	Discount Factor	Discounted Cashflow
0	100			–100	1.000	–100
1	90	10	9.500	19.500		
2	75	15	8.550	23.550		
3	55	20	7.125	27.125		
4	30	25	5.225	30.225		
5	0	30	2.850	32.850		

What is the updated present value of the discounted cashflows?

■ FORWARD RATE EFFECTS

In our previous analysis, we did not examine the impact of expected forward rates on MBS value. Because of prepayments, MBS cashflows depend upon the level of interest rates. We can now expand the analysis to develop some analytical measures of forward rates on cashflows and value.

Prepayment rates are driven by mortgage current coupon rates. Current coupon rates can be proxied by an intermediate Treasury plus a spread. A typical proxy is the 10-year Treasury rate. When creating a prepayment estimate, we can assume that the 10-year Treasury rate remains constant at current levels. Alternatively, we could assume that prepayment rates will be influenced by the forward 10-year rates.

To determine the forward 10-year rates we only need to observe the current par yield curve. From that we can derive the spot curve and from the spot curve we can calculate forward rates. That is, we could derive the projected 10-year rate in 2 years, in 3 years, and so on. (This procedure was described in Chapter 4.) Using these projected rates, we can calculate prepayment rates and solve for cashflows and spread.

Forward Rates

To keep matters somewhat simple, we will assume that our prepayments will be influenced by the one-year forward rates. Based on the starting term structure we can calculate the following implied one-year forward rates:

Table 8-11

Implied Forward Rates

Maturity	Par Rate	Spot Rate	One-Year Forward Rate
1	5.0	5.00	8.12
2	6.5	6.55	11.48
3	8.0	8.17	12.74
4	9.0	9.29	12.16
5	9.5	9.86	

The forward rate of 11.48% corresponds to the one-year rate starting at the end of year 2 and going until the end of year 3.

In order to demonstrate the combined impact of higher forward rates and slower prepayments, we will slow down the principal paydown used in the previous example.

Table 8-12

Cashflows with Slower Amortization

Year	Balance	Principal	Interest	Cashflow	Discount Factor	Discounted Cashflow
0	100			–100.00	1.00	–100.00
1	95	5	9.50	14.50	0.95	13.74
2	85	10	9.03	19.03	0.87	16.59
3	70	15	8.08	23.08	0.78	17.96
4	50	20	6.65	26.65	0.69	18.32
5	0	50	4.75	54.75	0.61	33.39

Using the same starting price we will recompute spreads to the curve and to the average-life benchmark.

The slowing of prepayments has shifted the average life to four years. The extension has reduced both the spread to the curve and to the average-life benchmark. Now, though, the spread to the curve exceeds the spread to a point on the curve. Once we extend the cashflows in this example, the average-life point of the MBS moves to a relatively flatter section of the curve. It's relatively more steep to the left of the average life than to the right of the average life.

Table 8-13
Spread Measures

WAL	4
Yield	9.50
WAL Spd	50
CRV Spd	53

Table 8-14
Change in Par and Spot Rates

	Par	Spot
Yr 1- Yr 2	1.50	1.55
Yr 2 - Yr 3	1.50	1.62
Yr 3 - Yr 4	1.00	1.12
Yr 4 - Yr 5	0.50	0.57

Table 8-14 shows the change in par and spot rates going across the yield curve based upon the curves shown in Table 8-11. For example, as we go from year 1 to year 2, the par curve increases by 150 basis points while the spot curve increases by 155 basis points. Our security now has an average life of four years, and the spot curve is relatively more steep going from years 3 to 4 than the par curve. This increased steepness helps to raise the spread to the curve relative to the WAL benchmark.

Now that we have computed the spread based on implied forward rates, we have two measures of spread to the curve: the zero curve spread and forward curve spread.

Table 8-15
More Spread Measures

Spread Measure	Spread (bps)
Zero Curve	87
Forward Curve	53
Forward Effect	34

By applying the forward rates to project the prepayment rates, we extend the cashflows along the curve. This negatively impacts the relative value of the security, reducing its spread by 34 basis points.

Forward-Rate Effects with an Inverted Curve

Let's consider the interaction of forward rates with a reshaped yield curve. We will use the inverted curve from Exercise 8-5. After computing the spot rates we compute the implied one-period forward rates as shown in Table 8-16 below:

Table 8-16
One-Year Forward Rates

Maturity	Par Rate	Spot Rate	One-Year Forward Rate
1	11.0	11.00	8.91
2	10.0	9.95	8.37
3	9.5	9.42	7.25
4	9.0	8.87	3.35
5	8.0	7.75	

Table 8-16 shows that for an inverted curve, the forward rates are lower than the spot rates. To judge the impact of the new forward rates on prepayments we will compare the forward rates in the inverted curve to those of the base case in the table below:

Table 8-17
Inverted Curve Forward Rates

Year	Base Curve Forward Rates	Inverted Curve Forward Rates
1	8.12	8.91
2	11.48	8.37
3	12.74	7.25
4	12.16	3.35

Exercise 8-6

What should happen to the projected prepayment rates in the inverted curve?

Exercise 8-7

Valuing Cashflows in the Inverted Curve

To solve for the spread, we have computed the discounted cashflows shown in the table below at different spreads to the curve and compared their sum to the current price.

Cashflows

Year	Balance	Principal	Interest	Cashflow
0	100			–100.00
1	90	10	9.50	19.50
2	70	20	8.55	28.55
3	45	25	6.65	31.65
4	5	40	4.28	44.28
5	0	5	0.48	5.48

Values for the cashflows above are shown in the table below:

Spread	Price Minus Discounted Cashflows
–50	1.929
0	0.625
50	–0.654

By using interpolation, solve for the spread so that the price minus the discounted present cashflows equals zero. In addition, what is the forward rate effect? What is the intuition behind the relatively large forward effect? Round the spread to the nearest basis point.

Exercise 8-8 (Advanced)

Taking the information from Exercise 8-5, compute the yield and spread to the benchmark WAL. Compare the spread to the curve and WAL spread. What accounts for the large difference?

Work area

Yield	
WAL Spread	
Curve Spread	

Exercise 8-9 (Advanced)

Derive the forward rates from the steepening yield curve in Table 8-8. What will be the impact on prepayments relative to the forward rates derived in Table 8-11? How will the changing prepayment rates relate to the change in the discounting of cashflows?

Work area

Years Forward	One-Year Maturity Forward Rates
1	
2	
3	
4	

Exercise 8-10 (Advanced)

In Exercise 8-4, we held the spread constant. Let's assume that with the yield curve steepening, the price only rose to 100.25. What is the revised yield, spread to the curve, and spread to the WAL benchmark?

Work area

Yield	
WAL Spread	
Curve Spread	

■ REVIEW QUESTIONS

What is the forward effect on IOs when the yield curve is upward sloping?

What features of a bond will lead to the greatest forward effect?

What are some of the advantages of using a forward spread for an inverse floater rather than the static yield spread?

■ ANSWERS TO EXERCISES

8-1

	Yield	WAL	Benchmark Treasury	Spread (bps)
MBS 1	6.00	2.6	3	25
MBS 2	6.70	4.6	5	70
MBS 3	7.10	7.6	10	50
MBS 4	7.75	12.8	10	115

8-2

	Yield	WAL	Benchmark Yield	Benchmark Spread
MBS 1	6.00	2.6	5.45	55
MBS 2	6.70	4.6	5.95	75
MBS 3	7.10	7.6	6.31	79
MBS 4	7.75	12.8	6.66	109

8-3a

WAL spread is 130 basis points.

8-3b

The spread to the curve is 79 basis points.

8-4

Early cashflows discounted at lower rates cause the price to go up, which decreases the yield and spread to the benchmark. The WAL remains constant because the timing of the cashflows does not change in this example. Incorporating prepayments that are sensitive to interest rate changes would change the cashflows. The spread to the spot curve was kept constant. However, the increased price resulted in a lower yield, which in turn resulted in a lower spread to the benchmark since the benchmark did not change.

8-5

Year	Balance	Principal	Interest	Cashflow	Discount Factor	Discounted Cashflow
0	100			–100	1.0000	–100
1	90	10	9.500	19.500	0.8939	17.43
2	75	15	8.550	23.550	0.8143	19.18
3	55	20	7.125	27.125	0.7454	20.22
4	30	25	5.225	30.225	0.6894	20.84
5	0	30	2.850	32.850	0.6615	21.73

The present value is $99.39.

8-6

Projected prepayments should rise in the third and fourth years as forward rates predict falling interest rates.

8-7

The spread is 24 basis points. The forward effect is 63 basis points. The large forward-rate effect is due to the significantly increased early cashflows being discounted at high rates.

8-8

Yield	9.72
WAL Spread	47 basis points
Curve Spread	87 basis points

When the curve was inverted, the benchmark WAL yield rose. This depressed the WAL spread. With a WAL of 3.5 years, a significant portion of the MBS cashflow is concentrated at the sector of the curve where the yields are low.

8-9

Years Forward	**One-Year Maturity Forward Rates**
1	7.143
2	15.157
3	12.818
4	12.203

In Table 8-8's curve, prepayments will be slower than Table 8-11 in two periods forward because the implied forward rate is higher (15.157 versus 11.48). The forward rates for three and four periods forward are comparable for both curves. However, since the curve in Table 8-11 is generally increasing over time, prepayments for that curve would be slowest in three and four periods forward. The changing prepayments will be reflected in the price of the bond.

8-10

Yield	9.41
WAL Spread	91 basis points
Curve Spread	102 basis points

CHAPTER NINE

Option-Adjusted Spread

Bob, the salesman from Bulls & Bears, had a favorite saying: "There are no bad bonds, only bad prices." He would use this phrase when trying to sell some securities that had some fairly ugly warts. There was the time he showed the PAC II with the paydown profile that looked like the humps of a camel. Susan generally felt there were some good opportunities in broken PACs and recombinations, but she needed a tool that could help quantify both the prepayment and yield curve risk.

She had heard about the OAS models but had stayed somewhat away from them. Everyone seemed to have a different model and they always gave her different results. However, even the corporate bond portfolio managers were talking about OAS for callable bonds. Susan realized that if the corporate managers could learn about OAS then this could not be too difficult. It was time to put on the rocket scientist garb again.

■ INTRODUCTION

Investing in mortgage-backed securities entails a fair degree of uncertainty. The future economic and interest rate environment is unknown and therefore the future prepayment rates and future security cashflows are unknown. Option-adjusted spread analysis is one method of dealing with the multitude of possible investment outcomes and summarizing the performance of the security.

Option-adjusted spread (OAS) analysis is designed to quantify the impact of the dynamics of prepayments on the value of the security. The method represents a simulation of the performance of the security under a set of possible interest rate environments. The interest rate environments must satisfy certain conditions in order to allow the analysis to produce reliable relative value analysis.

As with all analysis, option-adjusted spread has certain limitations. The strengths and weaknesses of the approach can be best understood through a detailed understanding of the process.

■ MONTE CARLO METHOD

The customary method of evaluating mortgage-backed securities is the Monte Carlo method. This method of valuation involves simulation of the performance of the bond under a specific set of conditions. Monte Carlo methods can be viewed as an extension of the valuation techniques described in Chapter 7.

First, let's review the four-step mortgage evaluation process and then apply that process to the Monte Carlo OAS evaluation. In the first phase, the environment is determined. For OAS, that means determining the rate paths to be used in the analysis. In the prepayment phase, a prepayment model, such as the one described in Chapter 5, is used to project the prepayment rates. In the cashflow phase, the cashflows of the security are calculated. For passthroughs, the process is similar to the analysis in Chapter 3 and for CMOs the methods of Chapter 6 are used. In the final phase, analysis, the cashflows are used to calculate various measures of risk and value, the most important of which is the option-adjusted spread (OAS). Other measures, which provide further insight into the value and risk of the security, can also be computed. These measures include option cost, effective duration, and convexity.

Table 9-1
Four-Step Process

Environment	Prepayment	Cashflow	Analysis
Create interest rate paths consistent with term structure	Generate prepayment forecasts using model	Produce cashflows for MBS or CMOs	Calculate OAS, option cost, effective duration, convexity

Pathwise versus Lattice Models

In Chapter 4, we demonstrated the valuation of fixed-income securities with embedded options using a binomial valuation method. For reasons that we will describe below, MBS are not easily evaluated in a lattice-based model. Instead, MBS valuation is usually conducted in a "pathwise" manner. By pathwise, we mean that an entire interest rate path is generated starting now and continuing until the maturity of the security. This path may be a single interest rate or a set of rates representing the full yield curve. Each path represents just one possible path for interest rates to take. A large number of paths are used to simulate the entire range of possible outcomes.

In the following example we show the connection between pathwise valuation and lattice-based valuation. We demonstrate that there is a direct link between the two approaches and that pathwise valuation and binomial valuation can produce the same results. We will use the same binomial trees as shown in Chapter 4.

Figure 9-1

The Binomial Tree Created in Chapter 4

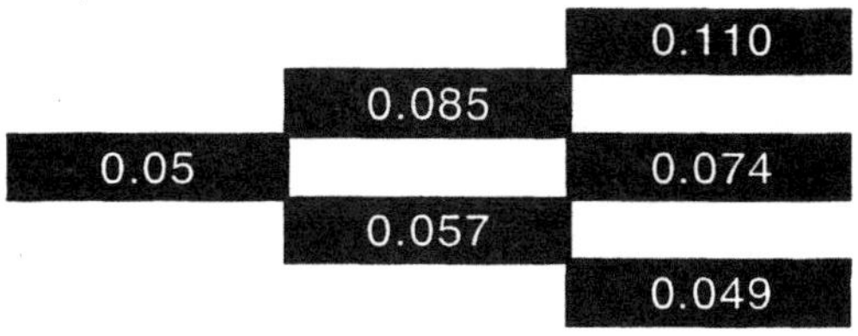

Creating a pathwise analysis:

Step 1 The binomial tree specifies all of the possible interest rate states over time. We need to establish a list of all possible interest rate paths through the tree. All of the paths start at the 5% rate. From there the path can either go up to 8.5% or down to 5.7%. Note that the down rate is actually higher than the initial rate. This is still called the down path. From either of these points, the rate path can go either up or down. Thus there are 2 × 2 or four possible paths. Generally there are 2^n possible paths, where n is the number of steps. For a mortgage valuation with 360 months of cashflows there could be 2^{360} or over 1×10^{100} possible paths! The fastest computers couldn't process that many paths in a reasonable time. Even if each path took 1/100th of a second, we could only calculate about 1×10^{11} paths before the mortgage matured! Table 9-2 lists the four possible paths and the interest rates for each path.

Table 9-2

Possible Interest Rate Paths

		Year	
Path	**1**	**2**	**3**
1		up	up
2		up	down
3		down	up
4		down	down
1	5.000	8.488	11.007
2	5.000	8.488	7.378
3	5.000	5.690	7.378
4	5.000	5.690	4.946

Step 2 Determine the cashflows of the bond for each path. Assume the bond matures at the end of year 3 and has an annual coupon of 7.5%. Since the bond is option-free, the cashflows are the same for each path. The bond receives a coupon of 7.5 in years 1 and 2 and receives principal of 100 and coupon of 7.5 in year 3.

Step 3 Value a fixed-rate bond using pathwise valuation. For path 1, start at the last period. The cashflow at the end of period 3 is 107.5. That cashflow is discounted back one period at 11.007%, resulting in a value of 96.8411. That value plus the 7.5 coupon received in period 2 is discounted at 8.488% to produce a value of 96.1174. That value plus the 7.5 coupon received in period 1 is discounted at 5% to produce a value of 98.7403. That value, 98.7403 represents the value of the security for the first path. It is the value of the security if you were certain that rates would follow path 1 (up, up; 5.0%, 8.5%, 11%) The same calculation can be repeated for each of the other three paths as shown in Table 9-3.

Table 9-3
Discounted Cashflows for All Paths

	Year		
Path	**1**	**2**	**3**
Cashflow	7.5	7.5	107.5
1	98.740	96.177	96.841
2	101.613	99.194	100.114
3	104.115	101.820	100.114
4	106.205	104.016	102.434
Average	102.668		

Step 4 The results of the valuation for each path are then averaged to produce an expected value for the bond. The average value is 102.668. Note that this is the exact same value as achieved in Chapter 4, Figure 4-5, using the binomial tree.

Evaluating Embedded Options

The evaluation of embedded options using pathwise valuation requires a different type of decision rule than lattice-based valuation. In lattice-based models, the decision to exercise is based on a comparison of the value of pursuing the strategy of exercise versus the strategy of deferring exercise. The strategy with the lowest cost is selected. In a pathwise valuation, it is not possible to fully evaluate both strategies, since only a single possible rate path is analyzed at a time. Therefore it is necessary to develop a decision rule that relies on information about coupon and current interest rate levels rather than prices.

The callable bond from Chapter 4, Figure 4-6, can also be evaluated using pathwise valuation. That bond has a coupon of 7.5%, a maturity of three years, and is callable at par at the end of year one. Here additional work is required. It is necessary to determine when the call option will be exercised.

Step 1 is the same as above.

Step 2 Working forward through time, determine when the bond will be called. To do this we need a decision rule. Assume that the bond will be called when the discount rate is less than 7.5% after the first year. Therefore the bond is called at the end of year 1 in paths 3 and 4. Table 9-4 shows the cashflows of the bond.

Table 9-4
Callable Bond Cashflow

		Year	
Path	**1**	**2**	**3**
1	7.5	7.5	107.5
2	7.5	7.5	107.5
3	107.5	0	0
4	107.5	0	0

Step 3 Value the bond as above, calculating the present value for each path. See Figure 9-5.

Table 9-5
Callable Bond Valuation

		Year	
Path	**1**	**2**	**3**
1	98.740	96.177	96.841
2	101.613	99.194	100.114
3	102.381	0	0
4	102.381	0	0
Average	101.279		

Step 4 Calculate the average value as above. Note that the average value is 101.279. This is the same value as in Chapter 4, Figure 4-6.

This analysis has shown that binomial valuation and pathwise valuation can give the same results for both callable and noncallable bonds.

Exercise 9-1

Evaluate an option-free bond with pathwise valuation using the assumptions of Exercise 4-6.

Work area

Interest Rate Paths

Path	Year 1	Year 2	Year 3	Year 4
1	0.0500	0.0694	0.1159	0.1703
2				
3				
4				
5				
6				
7				
8				

Coupon 8%

Discounted Cashflows

Path	Year 1	Year 2	Year 3	Year 4
1	94.7785	91.5174	89.8657	92.2840
2				
3				
4				
5				
6				
7				
8				
Average				

Exercise 9-2

Evaluate a bond with an embedded option using the assumptions of Exercise 4-7: Compare valuation using pathwise and lattice-based methods.

Work area

Coupon 8%

Callable at par after third year

Path	Year 1	Year 2	Year 3	Year 4
1	94.7785			
2				
3				
4				
5				
6				
7				
8				
Average				

Coupon 8%

Putable at 98 after year 3

Path	Year 1	Year 2	Year 3	Year 4
1	99.3404	96.3074	94.9880	Put @ 98
2				
3				
4				
5				
6				
7				
8				
Average				

■ REVIEW QUESTION

When will there be a difference between pathwise- and lattice-based evaluation? What are the advantages of each method? Can you think of a hybrid method, which has the advantages of both methods?

Issues in Path-Based Models

Using a path-based, rather than a lattice-based model creates opportunities and challenges for the analyst. One of the most demanding features of a lattice-based model is that the paths must "recombine." That is, the point reached following an up and then a down move, should be the same point as when following a down and then an up move. If the lattice does not have this feature then it does not recombine. A nonrecombining lattice does not have the computational advantages of a recombining lattice. In fact, it becomes just another form of pathwise analysis. Once freed from the constraints of recombination, the analyst is quite free in how interest rates change from one period to another.

Most lattice-based models follow either a normal or log-normal interest rate process. In a normal rate process, interest rate changes from period to period are additive. That is, rates change by a set amount for each step on the lattice. For example both the up move and down move might equal 25 basis points. It is easy to see that such a rate process will recombine.

Exercise 9-3

In a normal rate process, the standard deviation of the interest rates grows with the square root of time. If the initial interest rate is 9%, the yield curve is flat and the assumed volatility is 1.5% per year, at what time in the future will the probability of negative rates be greater than 2.5%? (Hint: In a normal distribution, there is about a 95% probability of events within two standard deviations of the mean.)

In a log-normal rate process, the interest rate changes from period to period are multiplicative. That is, rates change by a set percentage for each step on the lattice. For example, rates may increase by a factor of 1.20 for an up move or decrease by the reciprocal or 1/1.20 for a down move.

Exercise 9-4a

Show that a multiplicative rate process will result in a recombining lattice.

Exercise 9-4b

For a log normal process, if the step size is 50 basis points for an up rate move when the interest rate is 10%, what is the step size for a down rate move?

Exercise 9-4c

What is the step size in basis points when the interest rate is 5%? at 15%? at 1%?

Work area

	5%	15%	1%
Up			
Down			

Exercise 9-4d

What is the probability of rates less than 0?

Since the use of pathwise analysis eliminates the need for recombining paths, it is no longer necessary to restrict the interest rate process to those solutions for which recombining trees can be built. Some possible variations included are interest rate paths where the interest rate is proportional to the square root of the rate and interest rate paths where the rate process has a tendency to drift back toward some predetermined level (mean reversion).

"Path-Dependent" Cashflows and the Binomial Tree

Mortgage cashflows have the feature that the cashflow today depends on prior interest rate levels and prepayment levels. For path-dependent cashflows, it is necessary to say something about the history of rates leading up to today, not just the current level of rates or the prepayment history of the security, in order to calculate cashflow for this month.

The path-dependent nature of mortgage-backed securities arises from prepayment characteristics and structural characteristics. The prepayment characteristic that plays the largest role in creating path-dependent cashflows is burnout. Borrowers who did not prepay at the first opportunity to do so may face different costs of refinancing than other borrowers. Thus, past prepayments (and therefore past interest rate levels) affect our forecasts of future prepayments. Some OAS models are able to overcome this path-dependent aspect of mortgage valuation by splitting the mortgage pool into discrete segments with varying refinancing thresholds. Each segment can then be evaluated in a nonpath-dependent fashion. This approach requires that the prepayment estimates be constructed in a particular fashion.[1]

The second source of path dependency is not as easily overcome. This is the path dependence that arises from CMO structures. For many structures, future cashflows depend on past performance, particularly structures with scheduled and support classes. The past history of prepayments will affect future distribution of cashflows. For these structures it is extremely difficult to segment the CMO into pieces that are independent of each other and, thus, avoid path dependence.

Example: Path Dependence and the Binomial Tree

Suppose that at a particular time, say year 3, a bond can be called. The call price depends on prior interest rate levels. If interest rates have fallen below 7% then the bond can be called at par; otherwise the bond must be called at 102.

Binomial pricing requires that pricing begin from the maturity of the bond, and move backward in time. It also requires that a single price be assigned to each node.

In this example, it is unclear what price to place on the bond at node X. There are paths leading to node X where the interest rate has fallen below 7%. Therefore, the price of the bond should be 100; however, there are other paths leading to that point where the interest rate never fell below 7%. Thus it is necessary to assign both 100 and 102 to that point. Since both prices cannot be used to step back from node X to the earlier nodes, the binomial tree method cannot be used to value this bond without using a much more sophisticated approach.

[1]Davidson, A. S., M. D. Herskovitz and L. D. Van Drunen, "The Refinancing Threshold Pricing Model: An Economic Approach to Valuing MBS," *Journal of Real Estate Economics and Finance*, 1, 2, 117-130.

■ REVIEW QUESTIONS

Why can path-dependent features that are linked to balance or amount outstanding and interest rate levels be evaluated with a binomial tree?

Are ARMs path-dependent securities? Why?

Monte Carlo Analysis and Sampling

As shown above, pathwise valuation is more readily adaptable for path-dependent securities such as mortgages. However, pathwise analysis has the disadvantage that it is much more time consuming. In a lattice-based model, the number of calculations grows roughly proportionally to the square of the number of periods. This can be seen by counting the nodes. For a one-period binomial there are three nodes. For a two-period binomial there are six nodes. The number of nodes equals $(n + 1) \times (n + 2)/2$. The number of calculations is roughly proportional to the number of nodes. For a pathwise analysis, the number of calculations is roughly proportional to the number of paths. For a one-period binomial there are two paths (one up, one down) For a two-period model there are four paths and for a three-period model there are eight paths. However, the number of paths begins to grow quickly as the number of paths equals 2^n. Thus for a 10-period model, the number of nodes in a binomial model is 66 and the number of paths is 1,024. For greater numbers of periods, the number of paths soon becomes unmanageable.

Exercise 9-5

How many nodes and how many paths for a 30-period model?

In order to utilize the advantages of path-based modeling without bearing the computational cost of calculating billions of paths, analysts have developed a method of randomly sampling from all available paths. These methods are called Monte Carlo evaluation. A Monte Carlo method involves randomly selecting paths in order to approximate the results of a full pathwise evaluation.

One way of generating interest rate levels is to use a precalculated binomial tree to determine the rate levels at each time period. The Monte Carlo process then involves selecting whether to go up or down from the previous node. The interest rate level is then read off of the precalculated tree. Another method is to create a random interest rate path based on an equation that describes how interest rates change over time. If the second method is used then it is necessary to adjust these interest rate paths to ensure proper pricing of the Treasury curve.

Regardless of which method is chosen, analysts seek to find ways of choosing paths so that the paths are representative, while at the same time require the fewest number of paths. These methods are generally referred to as variance reduction methods. A commonly used method is the use of antithetical paths. In this method, for each path that is generated, an additional path is created that moves in exactly the opposite fashion. For example if one path began with the sequence "up, up, down," the antithetical path would begin "down, down, up." This technique serves to produce more accurate results with fewer paths. Many other techniques are possible.

■ REVIEW QUESTION

How does the antithetical path method work to reduce variance? Does it ensure accurate mean interest rates? Accurate cross-sectional volatilities? What are the features of a good variance reduction technique?

■ SIMPLE OAS ANALYSIS

In this section, we will construct a very simple Monte Carlo model to calculate the option-adjusted spread of a security. The calculations will follow the usual four-step process outlined below in Table 9-6.

Table 9-6

Monte Carlo within the Four-Step Process

Environment	Prepayment	Cashflow	Analysis
Create interest rate paths consistent with current Treasury rates	Generate prepayment forecasts using model	Produce cashflows for MBS or CMOs	Calculate OAS, option cost, effective duration, convexity
Step 1. Use additive interest rate process	Step 3. Calculate spread of mortgage to current rate	Step 5. Calculate interest and principal cashflows	Step 6. Calculate the price for each path
Step 2. Coin toss process to choose paths	Step 4. Look up prepayment rate in table		Step 7. Calculate average price and OAS

Table 9-7 provides the template for the calculation for each path. The OAS analysis will consist of a set of similar calculations, one for each path. Below, we go through the step by step process for each path.

Table 9-7

OAS Calculation Template

Period	0	1	2	3	4
Coin			Heads	Tails	Heads
Rate		9%	11%	9%	11%
Prepay		40%	5%	40%	
Ending Balance	100	60.00	57.00	34.20	0.00
Interest		11.00	6.60	6.27	3.76
Total Cash Flow		51.00	9.60	29.07	37.96
Present Value	100.62	59.68	57.24	33.89	

Bond Assumptions	
Coupon	11
Maturity	4 years
Vol.	2%
OAS	100

Prepayments	
Spread	Prepay
–5%	5%
–1%	5%
0%	5%
1%	15%
2%	40%
3%	60%
4%	70%

Step 1 Choose an interest rate process. Here we are using an additive interest rate process. The initial rate is 9% and the step size is 2% per year.

Step 2 Choose random numbers. Here we use a coin toss method. Toss a coin once for each time period. Record the results as heads or tails. Heads means an up rate path; tails means a down rate path. Our coin produced a result of heads, tails, heads. This produces an interest rate path of 9%, 11%, 9%, 11%.

Step 3 The prepayment model for this example is a look-up table with the input equal to the spread between the mortgage coupon and the discount rate. The mortgage coupon equals 11%. For each period calculate the spread.

Step 4 Determine the prepayment rate from the table. The spreads are 2%, 0, 2%, 0. The prepayment rates are 40%, 5% 40%. The final prepayment rate does not matter, because the bond matures in year 4.

Step 5 Calculate interest and principal cashflows. The interest cashflows equal the coupon times the beginning balance. The principal cashflows equal the prepayment rate times the ending balance from the previous period. The balances are 100, 60, 57, 34.2, and 0. The interest cashflows are 11, 6.6, 6.27, and 3.76.

Step 6 Calculate the price for this path assuming an OAS of 100 basis points. The discounting process is accomplished by starting from the last cashflow and then discounting backward. The discount rate is calculated by adding the OAS (in percent) to the current interest rate. The cashflow in year 4 is 37.962 and the discount rate is 12% (11% + 1%). The present value of that cashflow in year 3 is 33.89. The sum of the present value of the year 4 cashflow and the cashflow from year 3 is 62.96. The present value is 57.24 using a 10% discount rate. The process is repeated for year 2 and then for year 1. The calculated present value is 100.62 for this rate path. This process can be represented in general by Equation 9-1.

Equation 9-1
Path Present Value

$$PV_i = \sum_{j=1}^{WAM} \left(\frac{\text{cashflow}_{ij}}{\prod_{k=1}^{j} (1 + r_{ik} + \text{OAS})} \right)$$

Where cashflow_{ij} is the cashflow of the bond in path i for period j and r_{ik} is the discount rate for path i for period k.

Exercise 9-6

Repeat Steps 1-6 for the antithetical path Tails, Heads, Tails.

Work area

Period	0	1	2	3	4
Coin			Tails	Heads	Tails
Rate		9%			
Prepay					
Ending Balance	100				0
Interest		11			
Total Cash Flow					
Present Value					

Bond Assumptions	
Coupon	11
Maturity	4 years
Vol.	2%
OAS	100

Prepayments	
Spread	**Prepay**
–5%	5%
–1%	5%
0%	5%
1%	15%
2%	40%
3%	60%
4%	70%

Table 9-8
Price Given OAS

Path	Price
up up up	97.54
up up down	98.86
up down up	100.62
up down down	101.54
down up up	102.49
down up down	102.79
down down up	103.26
down down down	103.43
Average	101.32

Step 7 Calculate the OAS. Since there are three periods in which the rates can change, there are eight possible paths. Assuming a 100 basis

point OAS, the values for each path are as shown is Table 9-8. The average value is 101.32. This calculation is shown in Equation 9-2. The OAS level can be calculated for a given price through a trial and error method. Table 9-9 shows the average values for various OAS levels. If the market price equals 101.32 then the correct OAS is 100.

Equation 9-2
OAS Model Price

$$\text{Model Price} = \frac{1}{N}\sum_{i=1}^{N} PV_i$$

Vary the OAS in Equation 9-1 until Model Price equals market price.

Table 9-9
OAS and Price

OAS	Price
50	102.26
75	101.78
100	101.32
125	100.85

Option Cost

Option cost represents the difference between the yield spread to the spot curve and the option-adjusted spread of the instrument. Option cost is calculated using the following steps.

Step 1. Assume constant interest rates. Note that because the yield curve is flat, stable rates equal the forward rates.

Step 2. Follow steps 3 through 6 above.

Step 3. Calculate the OAS and spread for that one path.

Step 4. Subtract the OAS from the spread calculated in the previous step. That is the option cost.

Exercise 9-7

Calculate the option cost for this security assuming a price of 101.32.

Work area

Price	
Yield	
Spread	
OAS	
Option Cost	

Option cost represents the value of the options embedded in the security. Theoretically it represents the cost to dynamically hedge the prepayment risk of the security. Practically it represents the additional yield that an investor should require for a security with option risk.

Exercise 9-8a (Advanced)

Calculate the price of a bond as in Table 9-7 and 9-8. Use the binomial tree in Exercise 4-5a in Chapter 4 for the interest rate paths. Assume a bond coupon of 9%, an OAS of 100bp, and the prepayment speeds used in Table 9-7. (Round down the spread difference to determine the correct prepayment speed.)

Exercise 9-8b (Advanced)

Calculate the option cost assuming prepayments based on stable rates (5% short rate) but discounting with spot rates.

Exercise 9-8c (Advanced)

Calculate the option cost assuming prepayment rates and discounting based on forward rates.

■ APPLYING OAS WITH SAMPLE RESULTS

Once the OAS model is built and the ability to calculate every conceivable spread and risk measure is at your fingertips, what does all this information actually tell you? Table 9-10 presents the analytical results for various coupons in the GNMA 30-year pass-through market. The prices are actual market prices as of 25 August 1995, and the calculations were generated using Michael Herskovitz, Inc., and Andrew Davidson & Co., Inc., OAS and prepayment models. The prepayment forecast and average life under stable rates are shown on the right hand side of the table under "Base PSA" and "Base WAL."

Table 9-10

GNMA 30-Year Analysis for 8/25/95

					MARKET Spread Settlement 08/25/1995		SPREAD TO		
Agency	Mat	CPN	WAM	AGE	Price	Yield	WAL TRSY	Zero Curve	Fwrd Curve
GNMA	30	6.0	342	18	92-26	7.18	81	75	75
GNMA	30	6.5	343	17	95-16	7.26	89	84	84
GNMA	30	7.0	343	17	98-5	7.37	101	99	96
GNMA	30	7.5	344	16	100-14	7.49	120	113	113
GNMA	30	8.0	347	13	102-16	7.56	142	127	128
GNMA	30	8.5	350	10	103-30	7.58	147	137	145
GNMA	30	9.0	349	11	105-0	7.48	148	134	151
GNMA	30	9.5	339	21	106-6	6.99	101	89	116
GNMA	30	10.0	296	64	108-28	6.35	37	30	64

					OPTIONS ANALYSIS			RISK		PREPAYMENT			
Agency	Mat	CPN	WAM	AGE	OAS	Option Cost	Fwd Curve Effect	Dur	Convex	Base PSA	FWD PSA	Base WAL	FWD WAL
GNMA	30	6.0	342	18	71	4	0	6.2	0.2	99	99	10.5	10.5
GNMA	30	6.5	343	17	75	9	0	5.8	−0.2	99	99	10.7	10.7
GNMA	30	7.0	343	17	76	20	3	5.3	−0.7	116	103	9.9	10.6
GNMA	30	7.5	344	16	79	34	0	4.6	−1.2	135	128	9.2	9.5
GNMA	30	8.0	347	13	79	49	−1	3.8	−1.5	185	138	7.6	9.3
GNMA	30	8.5	350	10	86	59	−8	3.1	−1.6	274	190	5.7	7.6
GNMA	30	9.0	349	11	92	59	−17	2.4	−1.5	381	275	4.2	5.6
GNMA	30	9.5	339	21	65	51	−27	1.2	−1.2	476	382	3.0	3.8
GNMA	30	10.0	296	64	22	42	−34	0.7	−0.9	469	400	2.9	3.5

Based on Michael Herskoivitz, Inc., and Andrew Davidson & Co., Inc., OAS model and prepayment model.

Spread Measures

Three different yield measures are calculated. The first, spread to WAL Treasury, represents the yield advantage over a comparable average life Treasury. On the current coupon GNMA 7.0, the yield is 101 basis points over a 9.9-year Treasury. While this is a simple and easily understood measure, it does not capture the different yield spreads earned on the earlier and later cashflows.

The spread to the zero curve incorporates the shape of the curve and the timing of the cashflows. The earlier cashflows are measured against the shorter end of the curve, while the later cashflows are compared to longer maturity Treasuries. This measure is calculated by considering an MBS as a portfolio of bullet bonds. This means each period's cashflow is evaluated as a separate bond. The yield on each cashflow is measured against the appropriate Treasury, and the spread which produces the market price is calculated as was shown in Equation 8-2. The zero spread on all the GNMA coupons is lower than the WAL spread. This is primarily because the lower yield spreads earned on the longer dated cashflows have a greater effect than the higher spreads from the earlier cashflows. The flatter the yield curve, the less difference will be seen between the WAL and zero spread measures.

The spread to the forward curve incorporates an arbitrage-free framework in addition to the curve shape effect. The implied forward curve is used to generate prepayment forecasts as well as to discount the cashflows. Under a positively sloped yield curve, the prepayment projections will generally be slower than under flat rates. This is because a positively sloped yield curve predicts higher future interest rates. Higher interest rates generally lead to slower prepayment rates as homeowners have less of an incentive to refinance. This can be seen by comparing the "Base PSA" column with the "FWD PSA" column on the right-hand side of the table. The corresponding average lives are shown under "BASE WAL" and "FWD WAL."

The forward curve has the greatest impact on high premiums. On GNMA 10s, the spread to the forward curve is 34 basis points higher than the spread to the zero curve. This is due to the lower forward PSA of 366 versus 428 under stable rates. For discounts and low premiums, the zero and forward spreads are virtually the same.

OAS Analysis

After calculating the spread to the forward curve, one more major component of value must be implicitly evaluated in order to arrive at an OAS estimation. This is the option cost that reflects the loss in value resulting from varying interest rates and prepayments. The option cost, calculated using a Monte Carlo model, is the difference between the OAS and the spread to the forward curve. The OAS values on most of the GNMA coupons are between 70-80 basis point range.

The medium premium coupons, such as the 8.5s and 9s with an option cost of 59 basis points, show the highest OAS. These coupons have the highest volatility of prepayments. As the coupon reaches 10, the option cost decreases, reflecting burned-out loans.

The OAS level of an MBS can be decomposed as follows:

Equation 9-3
OAS Decomposition

$$\text{OAS} = \text{WAL spread} - \text{curve shape effect} - \text{forward effect} - \text{option cost}$$

where the curve shape effect is the difference between the WAL spread and the zero spread, the forward effect is the difference between the zero spread and the forward spread, and the option cost is the difference between the forward spread and the OAS.

Risk

The two risk measures calculated using the OAS model are duration and convexity. These numbers provide an indication of possible price volatility given interest rate changes. Low premium passthroughs have the highest negative convexity due to their proximity to the refinancing threshold point. The convexity of GNMA 8s is calculated to be –1.5, indicating an additional price change of 0.75% under a 100 bp rate shift. Therefore, although GNMA 8s may have an effective duration of 3.8 years, it is likely to behave as an approximately 4.55-year duration instrument if rates rise 100 basis points. Discounts exhibit much lower negative convexity due to the lower volatility of prepayments. The high premiums that are more burned-out also have a lower negative convexity.

These risk numbers can be used to calculate hedge ratios. A hedge ratio represents the amount of instrument B needed to hedge the price volatility of instrument A. A hedge ratio is calculated by Equation 9-4.

Equation 9-4
Hedging Bond A with Bond B

$$\text{Hedge Ratio} = \frac{\text{effdur}_A \times \text{price}_A}{\text{effdur}_B \times \text{price}_B}$$

Exercise 9-9

Assume the effective duration of the 10-year Treasury is 7.45 and its price is 102.75. Calculate how many 10 year Treasuries are needed to hedge 10 million face amount of GNMA 7s, using the table below. Do the same thing with GNMA 8s and 9s. How many GNMA 7s should be used to hedge GNMA 9s?

Work area

Instrument	Duration	Price
10-Yr Treasury	7.45	102.27
GNMA 7.0	5.30	98.16
GNMA 8.0	3.80	102.50
GNMA 9.0	2.40	105.00

Treasury Hedge for $10MM GNMAs:		
	Ratio	Amount($MM)
GNMA 7.0		
GNMA 8.0		
GNMA 9.0		

GNMA 7 Hedge for $10MM GNMA 9s:		
	Ratio	Amount($MM)
GNMA 7.0		

These hedge ratios are only valid for relatively small movements in the yield curve. After that, convexity effects would require rebalancing. Also, these hedge ratios assume parallel shifts in the yield curve.

The different aspects of risk and value in MBS can be quantified with various analytical measures. No one measure fully describes all the risks of MBS. A full understanding of MBS requires knowledge of all the dimensions of risk and value comparison.

■ REVIEW QUESTIONS

What is the best interest rate process to use?

What are the advantages and disadvantages of basing the Monte Carlo analysis on a lattice?

Which features of a Monte Carlo OAS model have the greatest impact on the results?

If two firms are offering the same security and firm A says the OAS is 20 basis points higher than firm B, would it be better to buy from firm A? What if firm A has a higher price than firm B?

If you want a low-risk, high-return bond, should you buy bond A with an OAS of 350 and an effective duration of 15 or bond B with an OAS of 90 and an effective duration of 3?

If you buy a CMO with a high OAS, and hedge it with treasuries based on the CMO's effective duration, are you guaranteed a profit?

■ ANSWERS TO EXERCISES

9-1

Interest Rate Paths

Path	Year 1	Year 2	Year 3	Year 4
1	0.0500	0.0694	0.1159	0.1703
2	0.0500	0.0694	0.1159	0.1262
3	0.0500	0.0694	0.0859	0.1262
4	0.0500	0.0694	0.0859	0.0935
5	0.0500	0.0514	0.0859	0.1262
6	0.0500	0.0514	0.0859	0.0935
7	0.0500	0.0514	0.0636	0.0935
8	0.0500	0.0514	0.0636	0.0692

Coupon 8%

Discounted Cashflows

Path	Year 1	Year 2	Year 3	Year 4
1	94.7785	91.5174	89.8657	92.2840
2	97.6652	94.5484	93.1070	95.9009
3	99.9596	96.9576	95.6833	95.9009
4	102.3117	99.4273	98.3243	98.7688
5	101.5387	98.6156	95.6833	95.9009
6	103.9310	101.1275	98.3243	98.7688
7	105.7950	103.0847	100.3821	98.7688
8	107.7007	105.0857	102.4859	101.0064
Average	101.7101			

9-2

Coupon 8%

Callable at par after third year

Path	Year 1	Year 2	Year 3	Year 4
1	94.7785	91.5174	89.8657	92.2840
2	97.6652	94.5484	93.1070	95.9009
3	99.9596	96.9576	95.6833	95.9009
4	102.3117	99.4273	98.3243	98.7688
5	101.5387	98.6156	95.6833	95.9009
6	103.9310	101.1275	98.3243	98.7688
7	105.7950	103.0847	100.3821	98.7688
8	106.8436	104.1857	101.5396	called @ 100
Average	101.6029			

Coupon 8%

Putable after year 3 at 98

Path	Year 1	Year 2	Year 3	Year 4
1	99.3404	96.3074	94.9880	put @ 98
2	99.3404	96.3074	94.9880	put @ 98
3	101.6812	98.7653	97.6163	put @ 98
4	102.3117	99.4273	98.3243	98.7688
5	103.2897	100.4542	97.6163	put @ 98
6	103.9310	101.1275	98.3243	98.7688
7	105.7950	103.0847	100.3821	98.7688
8	107.7007	105.0857	102.4859	101.0064
Average	102.9238			

9-3

Let T=Time

$2 \times 1.5\% \times T^{.5}=9\%$, $T^{.5}=3$, $T=9$

9-4a

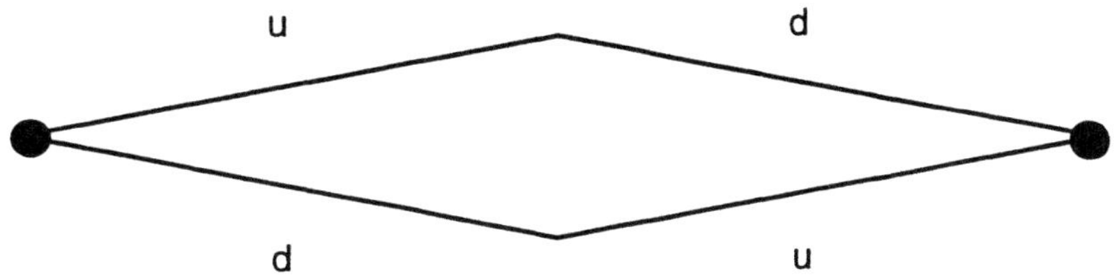

$$u \times d = d \times u$$

$$1.2 \times \frac{1}{1.2} = \frac{1}{1.2} \times 1.2$$

$$= 1$$

9-4b

The step size for a down rate move is 47.62bp.

9-4c

	5%	15%	1%
Up	25.0	75.0	5.0
Down	23.8	71.4	4.8

9-4d

There is a zero probability of rates less than zero.

9-5

There are 496 nodes and 1,073,741,824 paths.

9-6

Period	0	1	2	3	4
Coin			Tails	Heads	Tails
Rate		9%	7%	9%	7%
Prepay		40%	70%	40%	
Ending Balance	100	60.00	18.00	10.80	0.00
Interest		11.00	6.60	1.98	1.19
Total Cash Flow		51.00	48.60	9.18	11.99
Present Value	102.79	62.07	18.44	11.10	

9-7

Price	101.32
Yield	10.275%
Spread	127.5bp
OAS	100bp
Option Cost	27.5bp

9-8a
The price is 101.85.

9-8b
The option cost assuming prepayments based on stable rates is 49.2 bp.

9-8c
The option cost assuming prepayments based on forward rates is 13.8 bp.

9-9

Instrument	Duration	Price
10 Yr Treasury	7.45	102.27
GNMA 7.0	5.30	98.16
GNMA 8.0	3.80	102.50
GNMA 9.0	2.40	105.00

Treasury Hedge for $10MM GNMAs		
	Ratio	Amount($MM)
GNMA 7.0	0.68	6.83
GNMA 8.0	0.51	5.11
GNMA 9.0	0.33	3.31

GNMA 7 Hedge for $10MM GNMA 9s		
	Ratio	Amount($MM)
GNMA 7.0	0.48	4.84

CHAPTER TEN

Regulatory Measures

Susan's persistence and hard work were paying off. On a risk-adjusted basis, she was outperforming her peers. Susan was getting impatient, and she wanted to take on more responsibility. Bob, the salesman from Bulls & Bears, told Susan that the Bodyguard, a large life insurance company, was looking for an assistant CIO to cover the debt markets. Susan was going to try and get this job. She knew the markets and the bonds. As she soon realized, the insurance industry had developed their own investment rules. Knowing OAS was not going to be enough. She now had to enter the world of regulatory guidelines.

■ INTRODUCTION

The mortgage market has been successful because of its ability through CMO creation to adapt itself to a variety of investor appetites. Each type of investor faces a unique set of investment requirements through regulatory structure and investment objectives. Regulatory considerations have a large impact upon the type of mortgage products that can be purchased. Regulation of MBS is a tricky process. Ideally, regulations should guard against inappropriate risk taking either through ignorance or by intent. Judging what is "inappropriate," however, is a difficult task. Creating regulations that guard without making unnecessary restrictions on the sophisticated and capable investment manager is even more difficult. Two widely used regulatory measures, the FFIEC Test and FLUX, are discussed in this chapter.

■ FFIEC TEST

As part of developing policies of safety and soundness, the Federal Financial Institutions Examining Council (FFIEC, pronounced "fifec") has developed a set of guidelines to determine the riskiness of MBS. Depository institutions may hold "risky" securities but the securities must be reported as part of the trading account based on market value.

Alternatively, the securities may be booked as assets held for sale marked at the lower of cost or market.

As part of the test for CMO suitability, the FFIEC has instituted three testing criteria, as listed in Table 10-1. Any bond that fails one or more of the three FFIEC tests falls into the "risky" category.

Table 10-1
FFIEC Risk Tests

Base Cash Average Life	Average life of the CMO cannot exceed 10 years
Average-Life Sensitivity	CMO cannot extend more than four years or shorten more than six years based on an instantaneous +/– 300 basis point shift of the yield curve.
Price Sensitivity	The value of the CMO cannot change by more than 17% for a yield curve change of +/– 300 basis points or any incremental 100 basis point shift up to 300 basis points.

The FFIEC test covers many of the major risk categories which have been described in the workbook. It incorporates the notions of cashflow stability, as well as duration and convexity. For many institutions, considering these factors is an important step in the measurement and control of risk.

As a risk measurement tool, FFIEC has several limitations. Some of the faults of the test are listed below:

- The FFIEC tests do not consider the impacts of changing the shape of the yield curve. Key rate duration and twist measures could be used to examine this type of risk.
- Instantaneous interest rate shifts may be too conservative. Looking at volatility of this magnitude may not be realistic and could lead to disqualification of securities that are not truly risky.
- The tests do not consider the impact of interest rate paths. Whipsaw scenarios may cause a security to be vulnerable to cashflow variability as the rules of the CMO structures change.

Despite its faults, the FFIEC test does lead portfolio managers to carefully consider the risk profiles of securities they intend on purchasing.

Exercise 10-1

Using the tables below, determine whether the two bonds pass or fail the FFIEC tests.

Bond 1	FNR 1993-244 A
Date	1/12/96
Collateral	100% FNCL 8
WAC	8.472
WAM	313
Price	93-19

	Security		Treasury Spread		Security		WAL Change		Price Change	
Shift	PSA	WAL	Mat.	BP	Yield	Price	Actual	Max	Actual	Max
–300	632	1.19	1.19	62	2.749	96-27	–0.01	-6.0	3.5%	17%
–200	587	1.19	1.19	62	3.749	95-24	–0.01	-6.0	2.3%	17%
–100	515	1.19	1.19	62	4.749	94-21	–0.01	-6.0	1.2%	17%
0	335	1.20	1.20	62	5.750	93-19	n/a		0.0%	
+100	200	1.24	1.24	62	6.751	92-10	0.04	+4.0	–1.4%	17%
+200	150	1.39	1.39	62	7.755	90-07	0.19	+4.0	–3.6%	17%
+300	129	1.52	1.52	62	8.758	88-03	0.32	+4.0	–5.9%	17%

Bond 2	FNR 1994-45 D
Date	1/12/96
Collateral	100% FNCL 7
WAC	7.484
WAM	324
Price	92-25

	Security		Treasury Spread		Security		WAL Change		Price Change	
Shift	PSA	WAL	Mat.	BP	Yield	Price	Actual	Max	Actual	Max
–300	875	2.71	2.71	135	3.565	107-07	–7.98	–6.0	11.9%	17%
–200	800	3.07	3.07	135	4.597	105-04	–7.62	–6.0	9.8%	17%
–100	440	6.30	6.30	135	5.861	103-09	–4.40	–6.0	7.8%	17%
0	185	10.70	10.70	135	7.108	92-25	n/a		0.0%	
+100	140	13.26	13.26	135	8.160	87-05	2.56	+4.0	–9.0%	17%
+200	115	15.07	15.07	135	9.197	78-26	4.38	+4.0	–17.7%	17%
+300	103	16.04	16.04	135	10.217	71-20	5.35	+4.0	25.2%	17%

Source: Bloomberg Financial Markets, 1996.

■ THE FLOW UNCERTAINTY INDEX

The FLUX (FLow Uncertainty IndeX) model was designed by a committee formed by the NAIC (National Association of Insurance Commissioners) to provide an objective measure of relative variability of cashflows of individual CMO tranches over a range of possible interest rate scenarios. FLUX was created to assist insurance industry regulators in prioritizing investment portfolios for review and analysis. Andrew Davidson was responsible for the development of the FLUX methodology.

Measure of Cashflow Variability

FLUX measures the variability of the cashflows of CMO bonds under various interest rate assumptions. The measure has two components: a present value measure and a timing measure. FLUX is a measure of cashflow variability *not* a measure of market risk. FLUX does not measure risk associated with duration or spread changes. For example, a long Treasury bond (noncallable) would have a zero FLUX since its cashflows are certain. While FLUX is not a measure of value, it can be used by portfolio managers to determine the relative riskiness of CMO bonds.

Investors in CMOs face the risk that their investments will not perform as expected. While many total rate of return investors are primarily concerned about the market volatility of their investments, portfolio investors are ultimately more concerned about the cashflows generated by their investments. While there are many measures of bond value, such as yield and OAS, and many measures of price and return volatility including tools like duration, convexity and total return, there is little available to measure cashflow variation. Average life variability provides some indication of cashflow risk, but it does not capture coupon effects or the impact of changing cashflow patterns. Even measures like OAS duration are not truly measures of cashflow volatility. OAS duration takes prepayment forecasts into account, but OAS does not measure the risk of prepayments differing from the model assumptions.

Calculations

FLUX is specifically a measure of cashflow volatility. The FLUX measure is calculated based on the cashflows of the security. To calculate the measure it is necessary to calculate the cashflows of the bond in a base case and then to compare those cashflows to the cashflows of the same bond under different prepayment assumptions. In this way, the riskiness of the bond is calculated relative to its own cashflows. A present value measure and timing measure are calculated for each scenario. These measures are then summed for each scenario. The root mean square (RMS) of the scenario scores is the FLUX of the bond. Root mean square (RMS) is a technique from statistics that captures both the mean and dispersion of a group of numbers. It is calculated by squaring each number, taking the average of those squares, and then taking the square root, hence root mean square.

Floating rate CMOs require a slightly modified form of the FLUX calculations, which allows for cashflow volatility associated with coupon adjustments to the index. IOs and Inverse Floaters are evaluated using the calculations presented in this chapter.

Scenario Choices

While there are many ways of choosing scenarios, it is convenient to generate prepayment assumptions based on interest rate scenarios. The NAIC committee originally chose scenarios using a trinomial technique developed by Tom Ho of GAT. The scenarios that contribute the most to the FLUX measure were chosen. The current scenarios are shown in Figure 10-1. The base case assumes that interest rates remain constant. Under the six scenarios, interest rates move by increments of 150 basis points to nodes at 1, 2, and 3 years. Scenarios are: rates move up or down by 150 basis points, rates move up or down by 300 basis points, and two whipsaw scenarios. The committee plans to review the scenarios periodically to stay current with market conditions and developing CMO structures. The Public Securities Association (PSA) provides median dealer month-by-month prepayment speeds for various collateral types and coupons, for each scenario, once a year to be used in calculating FLUX scores.

Figure 10-1
FLUX Scenarios

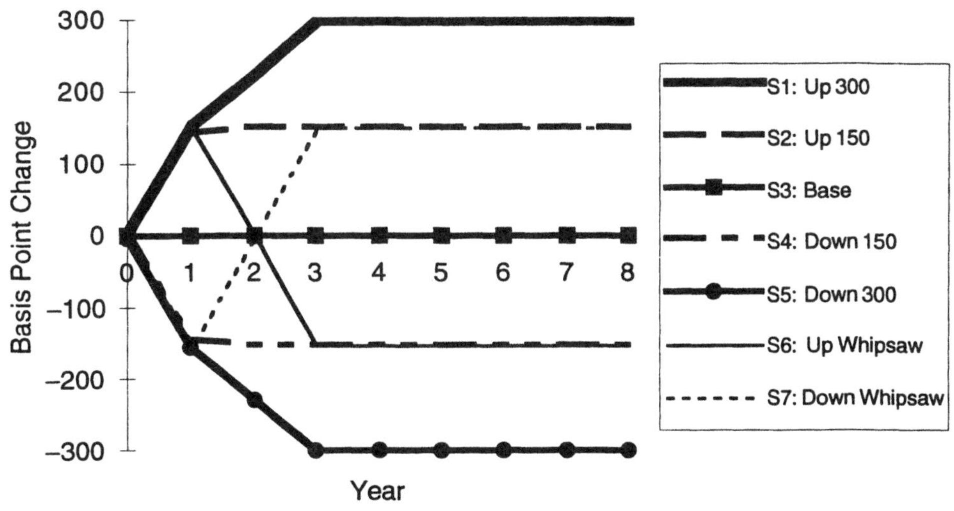

Present Value Component

The present value component is the magnitude of the negative percent changes in the present value in each scenario relative to the base scenario.

This component captures the risk of premium bonds prepaying sooner than expected or discount bonds prepaying later than expected. IOs and some POs receive high scores on this component. The timing component is calculated based on a period by period comparison of the cumulative present value of the cashflows in each scenario relative to the base case. This component measures potential reinvestment risk or asset-liability mismatch risk. Support bonds receive high scores on this measure.

The measure requires a discount rate and a volatility rate as inputs, which are announced annually by the NAIC. The discount rate should reflect current market rates on noncallable, high-quality securities, while the volatility should reflect the expected annual volatility of interest rates. It should be similar to the step size for the interest rate scenarios.

■ FLUX FORMULAS

1. *Cumulative Present Value* is the sum of the present values of cashflows for each month for each scenario.

$$CPV_{s,m} = \frac{\text{Principal}_{s,m} + \text{Interest}_{s,m}}{(1+\text{r})^m} + \text{CPV}_{s,(m-1)}$$

where m = the month
r = the monthly interest rate in decimal, set by the NAIC
s = the scenario

2. The *Present Value Score* is the percent decrease in present value from the base case scenario and is calculated for each scenario by dividing the difference in the total cumulative present values by the total cumulative present value of the base case.

$$\Delta PV_s = \frac{MAX\left(0,\ CPV_{base,\ M} - CPV_{s,M}\right)}{CPV_{base,\ M}}$$

where M = total number of months

3. *Absolute Scaled Differences* are calculated by taking the ratio of the cumulative present value of the monthly cashflows for each scenario and the cumulative present value of the total cashflows for each scenario. This ratio for the base case is also calculated and subtracted from the first ratio. Then an absolute value is taken of the difference.

$$ASD_{s,m} = \left| \frac{CPV_{s,m}}{CPV_{s,M}} - \frac{CPV_{base,m}}{CPV_{base,M}} \right|$$

where $CPV_{s,M}$ = cumulative present value of scenario cashflows
$base$ = base case

4. The *Timing Score* is the sum for each scenario of the Absolute Scaled Differences for each month each multiplied by yield volatility.

$$T\%_s = \sum_{m=1}^{M} ASD_{sm} \times V$$

where V = monthly market volatility in decimal (given)

5. *Scenario FLUX* is the sum of the PV Score and the Timing Score for each scenario.

$$FLUX_s = \Delta PV\%_s + T\%_s$$

6. *FLUX for a CMO* is a root mean squared of the Scenario FLUX scores. This is calculated by taking the square root of the mean of the squares of the Scenario FLUX scores.

$$FLUX = \sqrt{\frac{1}{S}\sum_{s=1}^{S} FLUX_s^2}$$

where S = number of interest rate scenarios

Table 10-2 shows an example of the FLUX calculations, assuming a 6% discount rate and a 1.5% volatility (150 bp yield volatility). The example is shown using annual cashflows, while real FLUX uses monthly cashflows. In the base case, the bond pays off fully in year 3 with a coupon of 8%. In scenario 1, half the principal pays down in year 2. In scenario 2, the bond extends to four years.

The cumulative present value (CPV) represents the present value today of that year's cashflow plus the previous CPV. For example, the CPV in year 2 in the base case is given by:

$$14.667 = 8/(1+.06)^2 + 7.547$$

The CPV in year 4 is equal to the present value of the bond's cashflows. The absolute scaled differences (ASD) are calculated by taking the difference between the CPV for the bond in a given year and scenario divided by the present value for that scenario and the scaled CPV of the base case. For example, the ASD for year 2 in Scenario 1 is given by:

$$0.427 = 59.167/104.506 - 14.667/105.346$$

The timing measure equals the sum of the absolute values of the ASDs times the volatility:

$$0.64\% = (0.001 + 0.427) \times 1.5\%$$

The scenario FLUX score is the sum of the timing measure and the PV measure:

$$1.44\% = 0.64\% + 0.80\%$$

The bond's FLUX is the root mean square of the scenario FLUXs:

$$1.3\% = \sqrt{0.5 \times (1.442\%^2 + 1.202\%^2)}$$

Table 10-2
FLUX Calculation Example

BASE	1	2	3	4
Principal	0	0	100	0
Interest	8	8	8	0
CPV	7.547	14.667	105.346	105.346

Interest Rate	6.0
Volatility	1.5%
Total CPV	105.346

Scenario 1	1	2	3	4
Principal	0	50	50	0
Interest	8	8	4	
CPV	7.547	59.167	104.506	104.506
ASD	0.001	0.427	0.000	0.000

Total CPV	T%
104.506	0.64%
Change PV%	**FLUX**
0.80%	1.44%

Scenario 2	1	2	3	4
Principal	0	0	0	100
Interest	8	8	8	8
CPV	7.547	14.667	21.384	106.930
ASD	0.001	0.002	0.800	0.000

Total CPV	T%
106.930	1.20%
Change PV%	**FLUX**
0.00%	1.20%

FLUX	1.30%

OUTPUT TABLE

	BASE	Scenario 1	Scenario 2	RMS
Present Value	105.35	0.80%	0.00%	0.60%
Timing		0.64%	1.20%	1.00%
Total		1.44%	1.20%	1.30%

The present value measure differs from other similar measures because the discount rate is held constant for each scenario. Effective duration and OAS measures involve changing the discount rate for each scenario. Here we keep the discount rate constant because we want to measure the potential for change in cashflows, not the potential for changing value.

The Timing Measure

The timing measure is a bit harder to understand, since cumulative present value and absolute scaled differences are new concepts. Figure 10-2 shows the cashflows of the bond under the three scenarios and the cumulative present value. From the graphs, it is easy to see that the cashflows change from scenario to scenario. The amount of cashflow changes only slightly, while the timing of the cashflows changes significantly. The timing calculation provides a numerical measure of how much the timing has changed. The CPV indicates how fast the cashflows are received. The difference in the CPVs reflects how much faster or slower the cashflows are received in the scenario relative to the base case. Cashflows received sooner than expected are subject to reinvestment risk. Cashflows received later than expected expose the investor to additional borrowing costs. The volatility factor helps provide an estimate of the potential impact of these differences in timing.

Figure 10-2
Cashflows for each Scenario

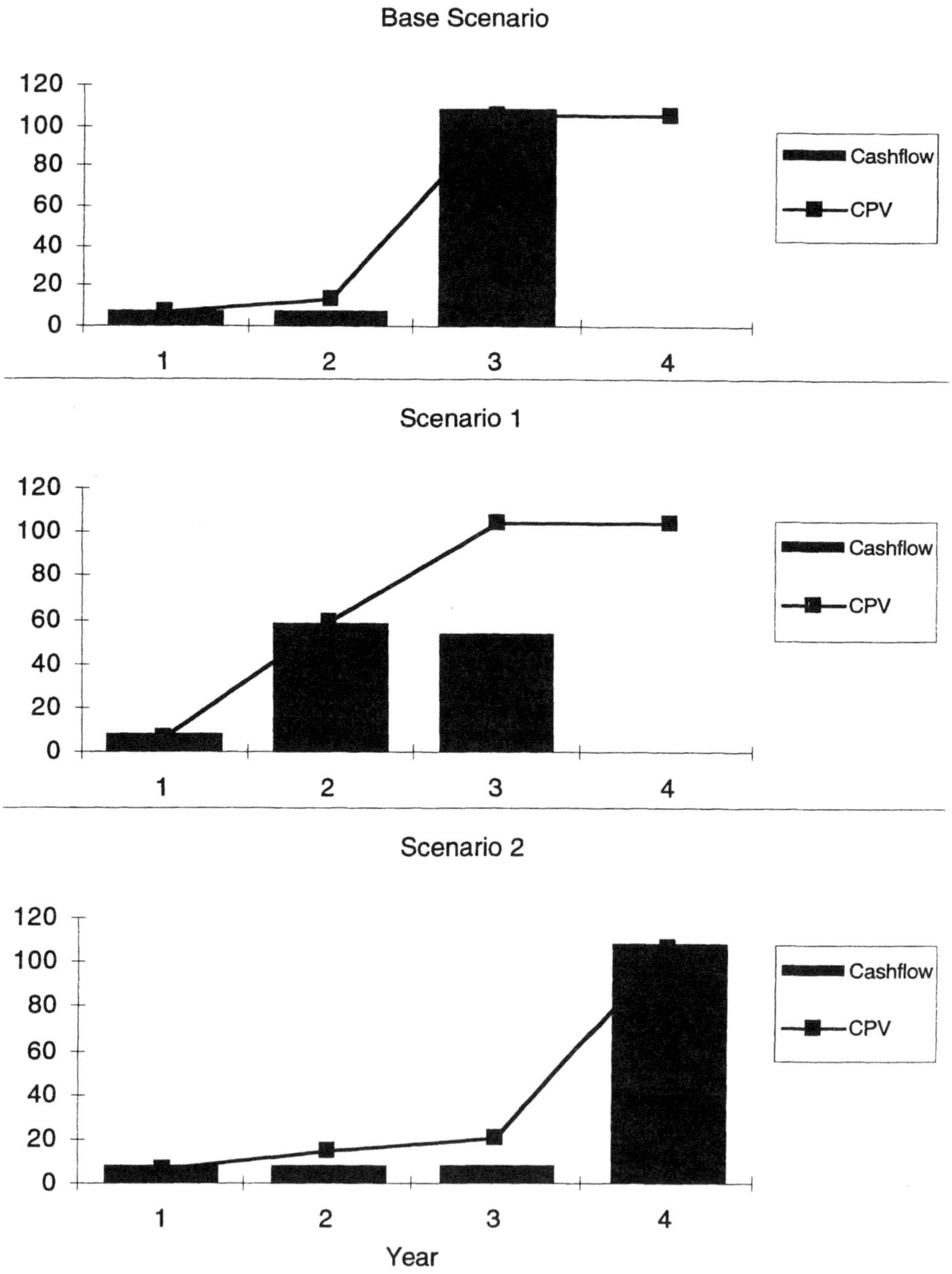

FLUX is a measure developed for the insurance regulators as a screening tool. It is a tool designed specifically to address cashflow risk of individual bonds. FLUX is another tool that investors can use to assess the risk characteristics of CMOs.

The CMO Cashflow Variability Project was headed by Chris Anderson of Merrill Lynch. Dave Hall of ITT/Hartford, Michael Siegal of Goldman Sachs, and Max Bublitz of Conseco headed subcommittees. Lutheran Brotherhood, First Boston, BARRA, Chalke/Intex, Bloomberg, and GAT were all deeply involved in the testing of model formulations and parameters. Numerous other people and firms have also been involved with the project.

Exercise 10-2

Perform a FLUX calculation based upon the following data:

BASE	**1**	**2**	**3**	**4**
Principal	0	0	100	0
Interest	7.5	7.5	7.5	0
CPV				

Interest Rate	7.5
Volatility	10.0%
Total CPV	

Scenario 1	**1**	**2**	**3**	**4**
Principal	75	25	0	0
Interest	7.5	7.5	0	0
CPV				
ASD				

Total CPV	**T%**

Change PV%	**FLUX**

Scenario 2	**1**	**2**	**3**	**4**
Principal	0	0	0	100
Interest	7.5	7.5	7.5	7.5
CPV				
ASD				

Total CPV	T%

Change PV%	FLUX

FLUX

OUTPUT TABLE

	BASE	Scenario 1	Scenario 2	RMS
Present Value				
Timing				
Total				

■ CONCLUSION

After finishing this workbook, we hope you will be aware of the rewards and the pitfalls of the MBS market. While multivariate regressions of prepayment data and programming OAS models may still be tasks reserved for "rocket scientists," we hope this workbook will enable you to have a basic understanding of the issues involved in MBS analysis. Our four-phase process, Environment, Prepayment, Cashflow, and Analysis, provides a starting point for investing in this complex market. This same approach can be applied to the simplest static analysis, such as a yield calculation, as well as to a complex Monte Carlo analysis of the impact of yield curve twists on a CMO.

Investing in MBS is a challenge for even the most sophisticated investor with state-of-the-art analytical tools and systems. In analyzing MBS, there are hundreds of decisions that you either explicitly make in building tools or that have been made for you in the system that you are using. Understanding your own investment objectives, the types of risk you wish and don't wish to bear, and the limitations of your analysis is the starting point for profitable investing in this exciting market. Good luck!

■ ANSWERS TO EXERCISES

10-1

Bond 1, FNR 1993-244 A, passes all three FFIEC tests.

Bond 2, FNR 1994-95 D, fails all three FFIEC tests.

10-2

BASE	1	2	3	4
Principal	0	0	100	0
Interest	7.5	7.5	7.5	0
CPV	6.977	13.467	100.000	100.00

Interest Rate	7.5
Volatility	10.0%

Total CPV	100.000

Scenario 1	1	2	3	4
Principal	75	25	0	0
Interest	7.5	7.5	0	0
CPV	76.744	104.867	104.867	104.867
ASD	0.662	0.865	0.000	0.000

Total CPV	T%
104.867	15.27%
Change PV%	**FLUX**
0.00%	15.27%

Scenario 2	1	2	3	4
Principal	0	0	0	100
Interest	7.5	7.5	7.5	7.5
CPV	6.977	13.467	19.504	100.000
ASD	0.000	0.000	0.805	0.000

Total CPV	T%
100.000	8.05%
Change PV%	**FLUX**
0.00%	8.05%

FLUX	12.2%

OUTPUT TABLE

	BASE	Scenario 1	Scenario 2	RMS
Present Value	100.00	0.00%	0.00%	0.0%
Timing		15.27%	8.05%	12.20%
Total		15.27%	8.05%	12.20%